STONECRABS THEATRE
BIAFRA TO ENGLAND
NIGERIAN HERITAGE PROJECT

Edited by Tanja Pagnuco

Biafra to England

Copyright © 2011 by StoneCrabs Theatre Company

The right of Tanja Pagnuco to be identified as the editor of this book has been asserted in accordance with the Copyright, Designs and Patents Act, 1988.

All rights reserved. No part of this publication may be reproduced, stored in a retrieval system, or transmitted in any form or by any mean, electronic, mechanical, photocopying, recording or otherwise, without the prior permission of the copyright owners.

Published by StoneCrabs Theatre Company in Great Britain
Studio B115, Faircharm Studios
8-10 Creekside
London
SE8 3DX
T: 020 8694 6472
www.stonecrabs.co.uk
This edition published in 2011 by StoneCrabs Theatre Company
Book Design by StoneCrabs Theatre Company
Jacket design by Chuka Odogwu
Printed by ThinkInk
A CIP catalogue record for this book is available from the British Library.
ISBN 978-0-9570364-0-6
Printed and bound in Great Britain.

«History is all around us, in our own families and communities, in the living memories and the experiences of older people. We have only to ask them and they can tell us enough stories to fill a library of books. This kind of history - that we all gather as we go through life - is called ORAL HISTORY. Everyone has a story to tell about their life which is unique to them. Regardless of age or importance we all have interesting experiences to share. Most importantly, historical documents and books can't tell us everything about our past. Often they concentrate on famous people and big events, and tend to miss out ordinary people talking about everyday events. Oral history fills in the gaps and gives us history which includes everyone. Unfortunately, because memories die when people do, if we don't record peoples' life histories they are lost forever.» - Rob Perks, British Library

CONTENTS

Preface	6
Historic background	9
Introduction	15
Interviews	17
James Adebayo Adesina	19
Dr Benjamin Akintunde Oyetade	25
Tessy Francis-Ilide	35
Emmanuel Odogwu	41
Nicholas Jamike-Njoku	54
Margaret Ilide	60
Dr Osita Okagbue	68
Felix Odogwu	79
Professor Herbert Ekwe-Ekwe	86
Paul Lanipekun	101
Acknowledgements	109
Notes, sources & bibliography	111

PREFACE

What is history? This is a question often asked, and one which has provoked various responses. At its simplest, history is what has happened. But how do we know what has happened, through what channels do we learn about it? Who is to say which events are central and which are trivial? Whose histories are we given, and whose are we not? And of those histories we receive, from what viewpoint are they presented?

There has always been oral history - the passing down of stories by word of mouth - and yet until relatively recently the histories that commanded the greatest respect in many cultures have been exclusively written histories. These written accounts of the past, usually based upon a wide variety of material, particularly documents, were produced by trained, professional historians. And because they were produced by trained, professional historians they were often assumed to have been somehow unbiased. But in fact historians, however fair and balanced they try to be in the presentation of what they shape into a narrative, in fact inevitably write from a particular social, cultural and ideological perspective. It is impossible to eliminate bias from our view of the past, whether the view is that of an individual looking back at his or her personal experiences or that of a trained academic putting together a secondary source of history.

For a long time oral history was dismissed by many in academia as the generally irrelevant ramblings of usually unreliable individuals. Well, oral history is certainly unreliable, but then so too are documents, since documents also may contain their fair share of omissions (intended or accidental), half-truths or plain falsehoods. Yet we often put a touching faith in the veracity of written documents, overlooking the fact that they, too, have only been produced by human beings. In recent decades, though, the contribution of oral history to our understanding of the past has been much more widely recognised, so that now there is certainly not a university and hardly a school in the country that does not use oral history as a valuable resource, to place alongside other resources.

To return to the original question, 'What is history?', oral history has contributed to a gradual change in what history has been seen as being. In previous centuries, histories were dominated by power and the powerful: history was the story of who gained power and how, what they did with it, and how they lost it. How so-called ordinary people lived, however – the day-to-day fabric of our lives – was of very little interest to the vast majority of historians until well into the twentieth century. That has changed. The rise in interest in social as opposed to political history has been supported by the rise of status of oral history, the recorded memories of people talking about their experiences. But oral history has not only played its part in altering what history is seen as being; it has also contributed to a change in who we see as historians. Being a historian is no longer the sole preserve of those specifically academically trained in the discipline, though of course such people continue to perform a very valuable service. No, now we are starting to see all of ourselves as historians, both in terms of telling our stories and as interviewers of others. Oral history has become a driving force in the democratisation of history.

There is another element of oral history which is sometimes overlooked: the language. The language of oral history is spoken, not written. Written language of course has its beauties. At its best it is polished, precise, elegant and considered, the result of a series of carefully re-written drafts. But it tends not to have the immediacy, the wonderful spontaneity of spoken language. And then there is the actual sound of the voice. I am very pleased to see that this project is producing not only this excellent book but also a DVD, on which the voices themselves may be heard. Oral history captures spoken voices - the intonations, the emphases, the pauses - and of course the specific vocabulary and accent that results from life in a particular time in a particular social milieu in a particular place. This is invaluable.

This publication is a remarkable one, exploring life-changing events through the words of those who have lived through them. The contributors look back on the rich complexities of ethnic, religious, cultural and political conflict, on the role of state propaganda and of beliefs that counter such blandishments; they pass on to us their personal, lived experience of post-colonialism and of adapting to life in the UK. These testaments are important, for Nigerians in Britain and those in Nigeria, as well as for the wider public. And they are particularly important for the descendants of all those who lived through these events, for, as one of the contributors comments, 'A river that forgets its source will run dry.'

Rib Davis, Oral Historian

HISTORIC BACKGROUND

Like many other African nations, Nigeria was an artificial structure initiated by the British which had neglected to consider religious, linguistic, and ethnic differences[1]. Nigeria, which gained independence from Britain in 1960, had at that time a population of 60 million people consisting of nearly 300 differing ethnic and cultural groups.

The causes of the Nigerian civil war were diverse. More than fifty years earlier, Great Britain carved an area out of West Africa containing hundreds of different ethnic groups and unified it, calling it Nigeria. Although the area contained many different groups, three were predominant: the Igbo, which formed between 60-70% of the population in the Southeast, the Hausa-Fulani, which formed about 65% of the peoples in the Northern part of the territory; the Yoruba, which formed about 75% of the population in the Southwestern part.

The semi-feudal and Islamic Hausa-Fulani in the North were traditionally ruled by an autocratic, conservative Islamic hierarchy consisting of some thirty-odd Emirs who, in turn, owed their allegiance to a supreme Sultan. This Sultan was regarded as the source of all political power and religious authority.

The Yoruba political system in the Southwest, like that of the Hausa-Fulani, also consisted of a series of monarchs being the Oba. The Yoruba monarchs, however, were less autocratic than those in the North, and the political and social system of the Yoruba accordingly allowed for greater upward mobility based on acquired rather than inherited wealth and title.

The Igbo in the Southeast, in contrast to the two other groups, lived in mostly autonomous, democratically-organized communities although there were monarchs in many of these ancient cities such as the Kingdom of Nri, which in its zenith controlled most of Igbo land, including influence on the Anioma people, Arochukwu which controlled slavery in Igbo land and Onitsha. Unlike the other two regions, decisions among the Igbo were made by a general assembly in which men could participate[2].

The differing political systems among these three peoples reflected and produced divergent customs and values. The Hausa-Fulani commoners, having contact with the political system only through their village head who was designated by the Emir or one of his subordinates, did not view political leaders as amenable to influence. Political decisions were to be submitted to. Like in every highly authoritarian religious and political system leadership positions were taken by persons willing to be subservient and loyal to superiors. A chief function of this political system was to maintain Islamic and conservative values, which caused many Hausa-Fulani to view economic and social innovation as subversive or sacrilegious.

In contrast to the Hausa-Fulani, the Igbo often participated directly in the decisions which affected their lives. They had a lively awareness of the political system and regarded it as an instrument for achieving their own personal goals. Status was acquired through the ability to arbitrate disputes that might arise in the village, and through acquiring rather than inheriting wealth. With their emphasis upon social achievement and political participation, the Igbo adapted to and challenged colonial rule in innovative ways.

These tradition-derived differences were perpetuated and, perhaps, even enhanced by the British system of colonial rule in Nigeria. In the North, the British found it convenient to rule indirectly through the Emirs, thus perpetuating rather than changing the indigenous authoritarian political system. As a concomitant of this system, Christian missionaries were excluded from the North, and the area thus remained virtually closed to European cultural imperialism, in contrast to the Igbo, the richest of whom sent many of their sons to British universities. During the ensuing years, the Northern Emirs thus were able to maintain traditional political and religious institutions, while reinforcing their social structure. In this division, the North, at the time of independence in 1960, was by far the most underdeveloped area in Nigeria, with a literacy rate of 2% as compared to 19.2% in the East (literacy in Arabic script, learned in connection with religious education, was higher). The West enjoyed a much higher literacy level, being the first part of the country to have contact with Western education in addition to the free primary education program of the pre-independence Western Regional Government[3].

In the South, the missionaries rapidly introduced Western forms of education. Consequently, the Yoruba were the first group in Nigeria to adopt Western bureaucratic social norms and they provided the first African civil servants, doctors, lawyers, and other technicians and professionals.

In Igbo areas, missionaries were introduced at a later date because of British difficulty in establishing firm control over the highly autonomous Igbo communities[4]. However, the Igbo people took to Western education actively, and they overwhelmingly came to adopt Christianity. Population pressure in the Igbo homeland combined with aspirations for monetary wages drove thousands of Igbo to other parts of Nigeria in search of work. By the 1960s Igbo political culture was more unified and the region relatively prosperous, with tradesmen and literate elites active not just in the traditionally Igbo South, but throughout Nigeria[5].

The British colonial ideology that divided Nigeria into three regions North, West and East exacerbated the already well-developed economic, political, and social differences among Nigeria's different ethnic groups. For the country was divided in such a way that the North had slightly more population than the other two regions combined. On this basis the Northern Region was allocated a majority of the seats in the Federal Legislature established by the colonial authorities. Within each of the three regions the dominant ethnic groups; the Hausa-Fulani, Yoruba, and Igbo respectively formed political parties that were largely regional and based on ethnic allegiances: the Northern People's Congress (NPC) in the North; the Action Group in the West (AG): and the National Conference of Nigeria and the Cameroons (NCNC) in the East. These parties were not exclusively homogeneous in terms of their ethnic or regional make-up; the disintegration of Nigeria resulted largely from the fact that these parties were primarily based in one region and one tribe. To simplify matters, we will refer to them here as the Hausa, Yoruba, and Igbo-based; or Northern, Western and Eastern parties.

During the 1940s and 1950s the Igbo and Yoruba parties were in the forefront of the fight for independence from Britain. They also wanted an independent Nigeria to be organized into several small states so that the conservative North could not dominate the country. Northern leaders, however, fearful that independence would mean political and economic domination by the more Westernized elites in the South, preferred the perpetuation of British rule. As a condition for accepting independence, they demanded that the country continue to be divided into three regions with the North having a clear majority. Igbo and Yoruba leaders, anxious to obtain an independent country at all costs, accepted the Northern demands.

During the late 60s and early 70s a large number of both Igbo and Yoruba communities immigrated to the UK as a result of the Civil War.

INTRODUCTION

Odoya Nigeria! StoneCrabs Theatre Nigerian Heritage Project was funded by the Heritage Lottery Fund (HLF).

As a Theatre Company working with young people in the area of South-East London, StoneCrabs Theatre realised the desire of young people to see more positive black role models projected in the community, and to find their identity reflected in contemporary Britain. Thus, in October of 2010, the project was born.

To celebrate 50 years of Nigeria's independence, StoneCrabs Theatre launched *Odoya Nigeria!* a Community Group forum to engage South East London young people and their mentors in educational visits to Nigerian resource centres such as the Horniman Museum, Museum of London and the Black Cultural Archives.

The project involved research and oral history interviews carried out in 2011 by a working group of 12 participants led by award-winning playwright Bola Agbaje, and workshops delivered to over 100 South-East London community members. The group carried out Oral History interviews, focussing particularly on Nigerian immigrants who have experienced the Nigerian Civil war. All interviews are documented in this book and in the DVD titled *Biafra to England: Nigerian Heritage Project* filmed with support of Mad Vision Ltd.

This book presents stories from professionals, skilled workers and immigrants who left Nigeria during that time and highlights their contributions to shaping the social and cultural identities of London communities.

Also, based on the findings of the research, Bola Agbaje has written *The Burial*, a new play which mirrors personal cultural conflicts imbedded in the political background.

As a culmination of this Oral History Project, a festival in association with the Albany, Deptford and Bola Agbaje took place at the Albany in London from 18 October to 22 October 2011.

The interviews presented in this book have been conducted by Chioma Ishiodu and Jennifer Maleghemi and transcribed by the group.

I sincerely hope that both this publication and the documentary will be actively used as a learning tool and introduce many more young people and their families to a section of history that has shaped Nigerian identity over the past 51 years. May it also serve as a tool to create discussion around the subject of war, violence and its barbarities, and how we can start creating a new century of peace.

Franko Figueiredo, Joint Artistic Director of StoneCrabs Theatre Company

INTERVIEWS

INTERVIEW WITH JAMES ADEBAYO ADESINA

James Adebayo Adesina was born on the 5th of August, 1934. He worked as a Technical Assistant for a construction firm in Nigeria and came to the UK in 1960 before the Nigerian independence. He lives in Woolwich and is now retired.

INTERVIEWER Can you describe your life in the UK when you came in 1960?

JAMES ADEBAYO ADESINA We came to this country on the 3rd or 4th of September 1960, full of hopes. At that time we thought it would be easy. You will finish one particular course and you will take another one. Maybe if you have 3 or 4 degrees you will go back to the country. It is once you are here that you understand it is not that easy. The impression we get from the missionaries back home is that everybody is nice and that they will be nice to you. But when we came to this country, there were big walls not easy to penetrate.

INTERVIEWER When you came over here was it mainly to study?

JAMES ADEBAYO ADESINA Yes, I came first to study and then I thought I'd return to Nigeria. And that was the desire of nothing less than 99.9 % of Nigerians who came about that time. We were still not independent when we came. We were self-governing but not fully independent. Our desires were to come back to our country to re-build our country, to take over from the white people who were administering us. So the desire was just to reach the end of the course as quickly as you can, pass the exam and go back. Not the idea of settling down at all.

INTERVIEWER What do you think made you stay longer after studying?
JAMES ADEBAYO ADESINA I was about 27 when I came to this country. As a bachelor then, I decided to get married. I got married in 1962. Then we had children. It is not easy to combine work, studies and maintaining a family at the same time. It's not easy at all. Money was not coming from home. What you work for is the money you get. You are going to spend it on your studies, to pay for your rent, to maintain yourself and the family. We were struggling all along, even for the things which are not as expensive as they are today. Many of us stayed here. You need to pay for the nanny who is looking after your children because you need to have a nanny to look after them, close to where you are living. Then you need to maintain yourself. You need to work. It is not that easy. That's the reason why it took - for many of us here - longer to complete our course.

INTERVIEWER Did you experience any cultural difference when coming over here?
JAMES ADEBAYO ADESINA Yes. Nigerians are outdoor people. We almost do everything outside. Even cooking. Dancing. Entertainment. We prefer to be on the road most of the time. In open spaces. But here, people are insular, they prefer indoor activities. And they are not accessible to make friends. Nigerians can easily make friends. I've been chatting to people who come here. If I am white, I will not open up to you like that. I will be a little bit reserved. But to me I look at you as my own. I will elevate you up. I will call you my daughter. They don't open up, they don't get together like we do. When I had my first child in the hospital, one of the nurses came one day and said "How many of your family are in this country? Because there's always a crowd in this ward". And that is us. We are very open, and we are very religious people so, maybe, that is part of what made a lot of us stay a bit longer.

INTERVIEWER How was your family coping back in the war?
JAMES ADEBAYO ADESINA We got news from home, from our family. Our relations. Here family is regarded as husband, wife and the children. Back home, we regard all the relations as family. We have amongst our family Igbos who have been there for years, Hausas who had stayed with us - even when I was in primary school as far back as 1943. We never called them by

their name. We called them Papa and Mama. We regard them as family. We got this letter from home that it was the civil war. The news arrived through the BBC and later a letter arrived at home. So it was very distressful.

INTERVIEWER The war was about tribalism and different cultures so how did it affect your relationships with Igbos or Hausas based here?
JAMES ADEBAYO ADESINA Most of us were a little bit God-driven, there was no dissension between us. We regarded it as a temporary set-back. But I will confess that to some people, especially the Igbos that were on the receiving hand, wanted to detach themselves from their very good friends. If you wanted to maintain good and cordial relationships, you skipped this discussion of the civil war. It is not for us to justify what was going on. When you look at what actually brought the civil war in Nigeria, it was a political problem.

The army did the coup and people were now divided into the North and the South. The Igbos thought their own fellow brother had let them down. But there is very little we can do as ordinary man. That is the situation. To me it isn't anything pleasant. And that has brought the misfortune that Nigeria is experiencing up to this morning. For something to bring division between people we learn with is pathetic. If there was no civil war and if we had come here and returned to contribute to our fatherland, Nigeria would have developed more. But the military took over. They are not born to be political or to be administrator. They are there to defend.

INTERVIEWER With the division that came about during the war, did you see yourself as a Nigerian or Biafran?
JAMES ADEBAYO ADESINA I see myself as a Nigerian and I also believe that the brother that calls himself Biafra would one day come here to be Nigerian. The civil war created that division. We believed that after the civil war was over, we would come back as one again. So, I don't regard myself as a Nigerian but I know it will be Nigeria for the whole country.

INTERVIEWER How often to you go back to Nigeria? And if so, how long do you stay in Nigeria for?
JAMES ADEBAYO ADESINA Since I went in 1971, I didn't come back except for holidays until 1994. And since 1994 to date, I stayed here because my wife was sick during a period. A very heavy sickness, we thought everything would be over. But it is not over. We are receiving some care here and I thought that as the husband I should wait and see her totally healed. That is the reason why I am still here. But we will go home every year, spend

two, three months and return. And all our children are here, so we always see our grandchildren.

INTERVIEWER You said you returned to Nigeria in 1971. Could you describe what made you go back to Nigeria in 1971?
JAMES ADEBAYO ADESINA East and West, home is still the best. And there is still room for development in 1971. Up to today, our mind is still there to contribute our little quarter to develop the country. So it is my home. But I am a registered citizen of this country. I became a citizen by accident. I must really confess. So I came here with a British passport because we were a colonial country, we were not yet independent. So when I finished my studies and I wanted to return home, I asked for a Nigerian passport to replace my British colonial passport and the official from the embassy kept on asking me to look for a guarantor.

When you are about to come to this country, you are going to a foreign land and you misbehave there, you get repatriated by the governement. The expenses of that repatriation is to be refunded by your guarantor to the Federal government. So there will be a letter, a document signed by a guarantor towards that. So that we keep in check to behave ourselves. The Nigerians don't want any bad name. So, many of us didn't misbehave.

When we became independent, we thought "why are we still having colonial passports? It is better we change to a Nigerian passport." So I applied and then they asked me to go and find a guarantor to sign for me.

And I understand that, if I'm coming to Britain and I misbehave, somebody must refund the money to repatriate me. But now, that I am going back to my fatherland, why should I find a guarantor?

That was the situation. So it is by default really that I became a British citizen. If they had given me the Nigerian passport when I was about to return, maybe I would not have had the citizenship. That's how I became a British citizen. Since 1971.

INTERVIEWER You said you went back in 1971. The war just finished then. What was it like going back home?

JAMES ADEBAYO ADESINA My family, my wife and my children left before me. They went in December 1969. They arrived on Christmas Day in 1969. And they wrote to me all the things that had been happening. My wife wrote me the full details, how the country had been devastated by the civil war. Things were very expensive or even not available. I stayed behind to be able to really equip the family with a few things. Things were very expensive. Things were not even available. And where I was working, the manager at that time asked me not to go back. You understand it is too bad. But it is my country so I have to go back. So it wasn't easy at that time.

INTERVIEWER What do you consider yourself as, a Nigerian or a British?

JAMES ADEBAYO ADESINA Both. As I told you before, Nigeria is a country I love, where I was born and Britain is the country I adore because today they are giving me my daily bread. They are paying my pension. I don't have to struggle for my pension. I went to the bank and by the time I collect my pension, it is in my account. I know Nigeria will reach this stage. But I will not renounce any of the two countries.

And I pray that the two of them will never be at war so that it never forces me to decide which side I belong to. I will be praying that there will always be cordiality between the two countries.

FOOD FOR THOUGHT
At the time of the war, how could James Adebayo Adesina, living in London, inform himself of the true situation in Nigeria?

Interview with Dr Akintunde Oyetade

Dr Akintunde Oyetade's full name is Benjamin Akintunde Oyetade but he likes to be called Akin Oyetade. He was born on the 1st of November, 1956. He teaches Yoruba language, culture and cultural issues in Africa as a university lecturer at SOAS in London. He is interested in the Diaspora issues.

INTERVIEWER Were you there when the Biafran war started?
DR AKINTUNDE OYETADE Yes, I was in Nigeria. I was about eleven when the war broke out, and fourteen by the time it finished. I was living in Lagos with an uncle of mine. We could hear all the stories about the war efforts, about people being conscripted into the army. Military people coming back from the war front were giving reports of what happened. At the time I was tall for my age and I remember thinking I hope I won't be conscripted to go to the war because I looked a bit taller than people of my age.

INTERVIEWER Were you aware of how the war started?
DR AKINTUNDE OYETADE I wasn't really aware, I knew that there was a coup and a lot of violence in Northern Nigeria. We then heard about this declaration of the Eastern part of Nigeria subsiding, and about the Federal government which cannot allow this to happen. We are one country and so

on. All you hear is a lot of propaganda on the radio, talking about the insolence and the pride of Ojukwu, who wanted to break away and take the Eastern part of Nigeria. When you grow older and you begin to read things, you understand that this is just propaganda from the Federal government and that the issue is a lot more complex than that.

INTERVIEWER What about your school, was it mixed with Igbos, Hausas?
DR AKINTUNDE OYETADE Lagos is a very cosmopolitan city where you have a lot of Igbos, Yorubas, not so many Hausas in the part where I was at the time.

INTERVIEWER Did the people from the East flee your school at the time?
DR AKINTUNDE OYETADE The ordinary people that I went to school with did not leave. There were stories of high calibre Igbo people, who were prominent in town and who probably thought that they may be vilified. I understand that many of them were not actually asked to leave, but some did leave and thought that they should go back and join the war effort.

INTERVIEWER What did you think about the government at the time?
DR AKINTUNDE OYETADE I thought the Federal government was doing the right thing, to fight and keep the country together. Because all the information you had, all the reasons for the war was received through propaganda, so you had no way of questioning whether that was the right thing to do or not. We didn't know exactly what the reason was for the war to actually break out. There is one thing that used to come out very clearly then, like a slogan on the radio. It was in English, "To keep Nigeria one is a task that must be done".

INTERVIEWER Do you think Ojukwu's government was justified to create Biafra?
DR AKINTUNDE OYETADE At my age I didn't really know any of Ojukwu's views on Nigerian politics. I didn't even know that Ojukwu was a very learned military person, I didn't know that he was a visionary. So what I thought as a child and what I began to discover as I went and read things, are quite different things.

Personally I think Ojukwu had a vision that Nigeria couldn't work with the way it was running at the time. I think he must have thought that you can't carry on this way, you have to do things differently, and if he had suggested it I don't think anybody would have listened to him. Not only because the presence of Northern Nigeria was so great, but also because those who just handed over the power, independent to us, the British government wanted it that way. I think it was in their interest to let the Northern people rule us. One reason is because they were less questioning than the Southerners, Westerners and Easterners. By the time Southern Nigeria was ready for independence, the North wasn't.

INTERVIEWER In that context, do you think Britain was right to intervene in the war and supply Nigeria with armies?
DR AKINTUNDE OYETADE I am not really convinced that they really passionately loved Nigeria for anything but for their own interest. If Nigeria can be kept together, it would be in their best interest, because before independence, Nigeria and other countries in Africa was just a ground for exploiting raw materials. If the whole place got disrupted by the war, it would not be easy to supply the industry here with the kinds of material that was coming from there. And Eastern Nigeria is only a section of Nigeria, so they were probably looking at the bigger picture, in saying that it is better to keep this region together.

INTERVIEWER What do you know about other countries supporting Biafra?
DR AKINTUNDE OYETADE The Republic of Ireland and Northern Ireland were really in support of Biafra. I think France was in support of Biafra, and when the war ended and Ojukwu had to go, he went to a French speaking colony of France. But I think there were more people supporting the Federal Republic of Nigeria than Biafra.

INTERVIEWER What were your views when the war ended?
DR AKINTUNDE OYETADE We heard it through the news. Leaders were serenading. You could hear of this surrender, and that the war had ended. Some of the leaders escaped in neighbouring countries. It was just euphoria, people were dancing and rejoicing in Lagos. We heard the Head of State, Yakubu Gowon announce the end of the war.

INTERVIEWER After the war, did the Igbos and the Northerners work together to rebuild Nigeria, or was it a slow process?
DR AKINTUNDE OYETADE I heard that there would be massive reconstruction, rehabilitation projects to reconstruct things that were damaged during the war. There was talk about it and there probably was a budget for it. How effectively those things were implemented is another thing. My experience with those kinds of things in Nigeria was that five years down the line, all the money had been spent on a project that had not been executed. Bridges,

roads, villages, schools and hospitals were destroyed but how much of that was actually reconstructed is a different story. I don't think they actually delivered as much as they talked about it.

INTERVIEWER Do you think that the Biafrans were portrayed well in the media?
DR AKINTUNDE OYETADE I don't think so; I don't think that the Biafrans were portrayed well. I think the idea of arrogance, even as a child I remember that "insolence", those kinds of words were used to describe Ojukwu, because he was just arrogant, he was an insolent man. These are the words that were used in the media to describe his actions, and his intentions of breaking away. I am not too sure it is as simplistic as that, but that's the way it was portrayed to the world. That is the way people saw it.

INTERVIEWER Do you feel that there is still a rift between the Northerners and the Easterners?
DR AKINTUNDE OYETADE I think so and I think it will probably continue for a long time. If you look at what has just happened in this election of April 2011, there are a number of people who were targeted and attacked in Northern Nigeria, not for any other reason but for the fact that they are Igbos or from the South East, and they are successful business women and men working in Northern Nigeria.

I have been reading a number of exchanges on the Nigerian website and on internet forums, and it looks like it is a kind of deep-seated problem, where I feel some sections within Northern Nigeria are very jealous of the success of Igbos, in Northern Nigeria in particular.

There are parts of Nigeria, particularly in the East and West or anywhere where certain businesses are completely dominated by the Igbos. Some people are very jealous that the Igbo people come to make their money, and are not using it to help the poor Hausa youngsters and children. To which the Igbos say "but your young people don't want to work hard, they're just lazy, they don't want to engage with the kind of things that we are doing".

I am from the Southwest, I am Yoruba and I know a number of people now who are beginning to reconsider whether they can actually continue to make Northern Nigeria their home. Many of them have lived there for forty years, some of them were born and grew up there, they are in their thirties and forties but now, those children are thinking, if their business which they have set up and worked hard for all their lives be wiped out in an instant, then it's not a place for them to be. So some of them are going back to Southwest Nigeria, even though they don't have any connection at all there.

If people have an ideology which says that because you are successful and you are doing well, we can't allow you to stay here and the way they do it is to kill you, and burn your house and destroy things that you have, you don't have any other solution than to go back.

I think some people feed these young people, these young boys with that kind of ideology; to see the Igbos and the Yorubas, who are living amongst them, who are not Muslims and who are successful business people as enemies.

INTERVIEWER Do you think education would be a solution?
DR AKINTUNDE OYETADE Education is gradual. The Federal government of Nigeria took a step in making sure that a number of Northerners have access to education as much as the Southerners do. Before independence, in the South we were exposed to a Western type of education but in the North they were exposed to Koranic education. Materials are older in Northern Nigeria, but it is also a question of mind-set that tends to look at someone who does not belong to your faith as a kaffa or infidel. That is actually strange in terms of other cultures that I know about in Nigeria: Igbos live in Yoruba land, and you don't have that kind of conflict between them. Also in the Islamic theology, if you are a Muslim you don't want somebody who is not a Muslim to be a boss over you. And that is a problem.

INTERVIEWER You mentioned Wole Soyinka. From what you know and read about him, what were his viewpoints about the war?
DR AKINTUNDE OYETADE He was against the war, in fact he has it on record that he was imprisoned because of his views about the war. In 1983, when he made the documentary about the transition of what was happening when Babaginda was Head of State, he made a statement that war should not have been fought, and he still believes that it was the wrong thing to do.

INTERVIEWER There have been talks about Nigeria going forward and Nigeria splitting. What are your viewpoints about this?

DR AKINTUNDE OYETADE Many people have talked about the best way for us to go in Nigeria is to split into our nationalities. I think if we want to look at it simplistically that is the best thing, but we have to realise that there are more than 250 linguistic groups. Actually there are over 500 languages and if the language is defined by the ethnic composition of people, we are talking about different nationalities. Nigeria is a conglomeration of people.

If I can borrow from Wole Soyinka's view, he said that he would compare the Nigerian state to a house that we did not build ourselves. Our British colonial masters built that house for us, and he said "we could do one of two things, we can decide to come together and live within that house, and set out the ground rules upon which we will live amicably in that house respecting each other, or we can decide to break it up and say look we don't want to live in this house, let people go do their own thing and break it up".

But the breaking up is not usually an amicable thing, where we sit down and say let's break up and we shake hands, it's not always like that, it always ends up in wars and fights and so on, and that will be followed by human gust.

You have to remember that 90% of the resources we use to run Nigeria comes from a particular part of Nigeria. So they will probably be happier there: the international companies will come and exploit the oil and that will be a more prosperous part of Nigeria. But what will happen to the rest of the country?

I am very confident that many powerful nations including Britain and France will be happy if the break-up happens because they will line up to supply arms to destroy us. And once destruction finishes they will line up to come and rebuild. We will be the losers. I think it is better for us to think as Africans, look at where our difficulties are and try to sort it out. We will lose out if we try to go by the way of war.

INTERVIEWER When and why did you come to London, and what were your experiences when you came?

DR AKINTUNDE OYETADE I finished my first degree in 1980 in the University of Ife, which is now called Oba Femi Awolowo University in Nigeria. I then started teaching at Adeyemi College of Education, I did my national service in Lagos and then I started working in the department of languages and cultures of Africa in the department of African literature and African languages and literature in Ife. It was from there that I came actually to London to study at SOAS in 1983. I did a diploma, then a post graduate diploma and then a PHD in linguistics, and then I went back to work at Ife in Nigeria. Ife actually sponsored me to come here. I then went back to Nigeria and worked with them for a couple of years. Later, there was an opening for a job in London, I applied and got the job. I came back here in 1990.

INTERVIEWER What were your experiences with moving and living in London?
DR AKINTUNDE OYETADE I was 27 years old, I had never been to any other place. I came in the autumn because it was the beginning of the session. I was not properly dressed for the weather, and there were those autumn winds. I booked a place in Paddington, it was called Lillian Benson Hall, I thought we had a room, we got a taxi and when we got there, they had closed for the day so there was no place to stay. I was really disappointed but we managed to get a hotel room nearby and we stayed there overnight. I was really impressed by the organisation of the city, I had never seen an underground before. It was marvellous.

My experiences as a student are completely different to my experiences when I came here to work. It's quite a different thing entirely. I was sponsored by the University of Nigeria to do well, but of course I brought my wife along and we later found out that she was expecting our first child. That was a difficult thing. I didn't really factor in the cultural differences. If you were in Nigeria and you are going to school, and you are going to have children then you have parents to rely on and relatives and people to help. But here, it really disrupted our plans: we were kicked out of the hall because it was not made for people who were expecting babies. So we had to start looking for a place in Islington, and later in Hackney.

INTERVIEWER Did you experience any prejudice at all?
DR AKINTUNDE OYETADE Yes I did, I experienced some form of discrimination as a student. I was 27 years old and I had done my first degree, I had started to work as a lecturer in Nigeria. To survive, at times, I had to take on a part-time job. The money that I received to maintain myself and my school fees would not come at the right time. And I had a wife and a son to look after. The job I considered to be better for me was a security guard. I found that when I was posted to jobs, I had to be managed by people who had hardly finished their GCSE. I had to challenge that because some of them are really very ignorant, they assume that because you are a black person doing a security job, that's all you are doing. I had to really fight.

I liked the security jobs because if you have the physical stature that can make people respect you, then they don't mess with you. I can sit down there and when it is quiet, I can read my book. That's the reason why I chose that. It worked for me.

INTERVIEWER What do you think is the role of people living in the Diaspora in developing Nigeria?

DR AKINTUNDE OYETADE I think we have many roles to play in developing Nigeria. Every time I go to Nigeria, I see the level of development, it's nothing to compare with what we enjoy here but I think that should not be the reason why we should just abandon our people there.

We know of things that work here, we know good practice here and it may be very difficult because we are not in the position of power, we are not in government to change things over night, but we can impact that on people.

I think we are lucky that we are gradually getting to a situation where we are having what we call democratic government, no matter how imperfect that is, it's better than being led by the military or a dictatorship. People are beginning to demand results, they are beginning to say "you promised this when you wanted to be elected, what have you delivered?". And that's where we come in, we can begin to ask people to vote for people who have ideas, who want to actually do things in their environment.

I don't think it is acceptable to go to any place in Nigeria where they don't have good drinking water. People are still dying of so many diseases related to poor water and sanitation issues. Some of the roads are bad. There is a power shortage most of the time so people can't even do profitable business if it has to rely on electricity. These things I believe will change because the luxury we enjoy here wasn't built in a day. But we need people who are accountable, who are accountable to you, to the people who have voted them into power.

There is a lot of money in Nigeria but the people are very selfish and take this money for personal, individual use. A particular contractor takes money to do a road, and people know that they collect that money but the road is not done and they still live in that society. That should not be acceptable. People should not live with that anymore, because nobody is benefiting from that. So our role is to interact. Don't stay here because you live in London and Nigeria has a lot of mosquitos so you don't want to go. No. Go there and interact with people, show them how things can be different and hopefully we will get there. I am a passionate believer in this.

INTERVIEWER Would you consider yourself British or Nigerian?
DR AKINTUNDE OYETADE I am first and foremost Nigerian, I have lived in Britain enough to be called British as well, and I have the British citizenship but my heart is in Nigeria. But I am living here. East or West, home is the best.

INTERVIEWER Would your kids consider themselves to be British or Nigerian if we were to ask them?
DR AKINTUNDE OYETADE They consider themselves to be British because they were born here, but I make sure they all have Nigerian passports. Although they were not born in Nigeria, it is allowed. They consider themselves Nigerians but also British, but I think they tend to be more British than Nigerian.

INTERVIEWER Why is it so important for a British person to know about where they come from?
DR AKINTUNDE OYETADE There is a saying, it's a Yoruba saying that says "Odo to ba bari ere sun re e o gbe" that is "A river that forgets its source will run dry". I think I rest my case.

FOOD FOR THOUGHT

What are the things that you think Nigeria could benefit from in the way we live here in Britain? And what do you think we could benefit from in the way Nigerians live?

In what way could the arrogance of the powerful be related to the despair of the powerless? How can you develop genuine confidence when facing difficulties or feeling powerless?

How should we deal with people who display arrogant attitudes? Moreover, how can we develop ourselves not to mistake other's confidence for arrogance and our arrogance for confidence?

Freddick Ilide in london in the 1960s (Husband of Margaret Ilide)

INTERVIEW WITH TESSY FRANCIS

Tessy Francis-Ilide was born on the 28th of March, 1961 in Nigeria. She is a Housing Officer and a Business woman.

INTERVIEWER Could you tell me about your early childhood memories of Nigeria?

TESSY FRANCIS My early childhood memories of Nigeria are quite vivid. I was six years old when the Biafran war started. We had to move from Lagos to the village and went back to Ashaka, with my mom and my other siblings. Because we came from the Igbo-speaking area, we were part of the Biafran people. The Nigerian soldiers came and flooded the area. I remember as a child each time they came into the town, we could hear loud noises and we'd have to run towards the other village, like running outside the town. Everybody was running, people were falling down, afraid of what was going to happen. I can recall the sound of the children. That was quite frightening.

INTERVIEWER Do you remember when the war was going on, what were you and your family doing?

TESSY FRANCIS My mom returned from the United Kingdom, she was a Fashion Designer, she was busy sewing clothes for the college. We didn't go to school much, because nothing was really happening in schools. They were shut. We were alone with my mum, helping with the house and helping her in what she was doing. I remember our house was right opposite the market in Ashaka. We were just playing and running around and hoping for the best.

INTERVIEWER Did you see people dying around you?
TESSY FRANCIS My mum was very protective of us. We had a big compound where when there was any kind of attack, we were all running to the compound and hiding there until the whole chaos was over. But I remember there was an incident when I was sent to the stream, to fetch some water from the stream. On my way I saw the Nigerian army. I decided to peep and see what was going on. And as I looked in, they had this long cane made from a cow - kind of leather. Cow leather. And they were using the skin to beat these people. As I peeped in, the tail of the cane went on the back of my hand and the skin came off. I was bleeding, I was crying, I had to run, I didn't go to the stream anymore, I had to run back to the house. When I got back my mum was quite upset. She said: "you were sent to do something. You're so naughty. You went instead doing something else." This occasionally happened. I didn't really see dead bodies, but there was a lot of chaos, there were people running here and there and going from one village to the other.

INTERVIEWER In terms of aid and food coming in, were you lacking in any way?
TESSY FRANCIS We didn't really lack - initially there was food and the market was going on, as usual. But when we heard shooting and people were running, falling, we had supplies of food - to a great extent.

INTERVIEWER Do you remember anything in particular about the end of the war?
TESSY FRANCIS When the war stopped, the whole place was in a mess. People didn't know what to do. A lot of people were frightened. Some people lost their families. Some people lost their livelihood. The schools were closed. It took a while for things to get back to normal. And as a kid, I suppose we're just filling in the space, running around, hoping everything will come back to normal and that we'd return to school.

INTERVIEWER At that age, did you have any knowledge if you were for Biafra or Nigeria?
TESSY FRANCIS We were deemed part of the Biafran people, because we came from the Igbo-speaking area. And I remember one incident when the

Nigerian army invaded the town. The Northern soldiers, they deemed us to be Biafrans because of our language and wanted to start treating us as the Biafran people, but we were then for Nigeria, not for Biafra. It was quite confusing. People got scared and they were worried that they might start killing us like the Biafran people. I remember they were quite upset with people from my area, because there was a lot of trade going on there. And during that period, the trade of salt was deemed contraband and it was punishable by death if anybody was seen trying to aid the Biafran people with any of such items as salt. When they were caught I suppose they were killed.

INTERVIEWER When you were going to school, was there any difference between you and the Northern children?
TESSY FRANCIS There was no difference. We were in the school together as one. There was no separation or anything of that nature.

INTERVIEWER When Ojukwu fled Nigeria, were people upset that he had left the Biafrans to deal with the aftermath of the war?
TESSY FRANCIS During the war, I was six years old. I only heard what the adults were saying. There wasn't much news going on, like television or radio. We were supposed to be Nigerians, not part of the Biafra, so whatever happened within the Biafran sector wasn't really our concern to an extent. We were more concerned about our well-being. And we didn't want a situation where we were grouped or classified as Biafrans, because we were on the side of the Nigerians. I wasn't really interested in what was going on. I was just worried for my safety and the safety of my family.

Above: Theresa Ilide-Francis on her 50th birthday (Recent)
Below: Tokunbo Ilide (Sister), Theresa Ilide-Francis, Subola Olowokere (Sister) in Nigeria

*The family at the airport on their way to Italy on a vacation
From left to right: Margaret Ilide (Grandmother), Jennifer Maleghemi (Daughter), Theresa Ilide-Francis*

INTERVIEWER When and why did you come to England?

TESSY FRANCIS Initially after the war we went back to Lagos, I continued school and then I started working. The first time I came to England I was 18 years old. I came on a visit. I heard a lot about England so I came. I came on a holiday visit. I then went back to Nigeria and once my business was established in Nigeria, I moved over here for a period. I came in 1991 and stayed for about six months but then I just decided to stay on.

INTERVIEWER And what were your experiences when you first came? Did you experience any prejudice?

TESSY FRANCIS My dad came to study, my mum came to join my dad and all they did then was schooling, because people came here to study. I didn't really know that Nigerians came here to work and do minor jobs and all that. So, I came likewise in the same manner, I came with some money. And after six months when I decided to stay, my friends told me that I had to engage in some form of work. I was quite blessed, because I did. It wasn't difficult for me. I was introduced to an agency and worked with the Camden Council. It was good. Personally my experience wasn't difficult. I was blessed.

INTERVIEWER Would you describe yourself as Nigerian or British?

TESSY FRANCIS Now we are privileged to hold dual nationality. So, I suppose I am Nigerian as well as British.

INTERVIEWER And what would your daughter class herself as, British or Nigerian?

TESSY FRANCIS It is up to her. She is privileged to hold dual nationality, so she can either class herself as Nigerian or British.

INTERVIEWER And going back to Nigeria, how far do you think Nigeria has developed since gaining its independence and getting to where it is now in 2011?

TESSY FRANCIS There was a lot of stability on how things were run at that time: we had good shops, we had movies. But suddenly with the Biafran war, everything crushed, and our people had to struggle for a lot of things. Apart from those who were privileged to travel outside of the country to acquire whatever they needed to acquire. I can say I was privileged to be one of those.

In terms of development, Nigeria has moved gradually through a reconstructive period. Things have improved, so it has been a gradual process. In the last elections it was quite impressive. Nigeria portrayed that it had matured from what has been going on over the years. The election was quite credible and the whole world saw Nigeria as a nation that has come up to the standard they are supposed to portray. So I'm quite happy with what's going on in Nigeria. This present government has been given the chance to rule peacefully with the support of Nigerians.

I see Nigeria as a great nation but it requires support from all Nigerians to work together, to bring the nation back to where it used to be. We have resources, we have resourceful men and women, skilled entrepreneurs, so it's a question of all of us coming together and supporting the present government to build Nigeria, to become a better Nigeria, where all the nations will be able to associate with us, do business with us, and move forward.

Everybody now, and although we've been here for some twenty years, we are looking forward to going back to Nigeria: a great Nigeria, where everything is in place, and especially where the electricity is working, which is one of the main reasons why business is not yet affluent in that country. No external investor wants to invest in a nation where there is no electricity. Electricity plays a vital role in industry, so as a businessperson I look forward to going back to Nigeria, where the infrastructure is in place and things are working and running smoothly.

FOOD FOR THOUGHT
Competition drives society. But why are some competitive people successful yet insecure ? What is the weakness of a life built upon a sense of superiority ?

Interview with Emmanuel Odogwu

Emmanuel Odogwu was born in Sapele, Nigeria, in the Delta area of the old Nigerian Mid-West state on 16th of March, 1946. He was entitled local chief in Nigeria and his title name is Ogbueshi Emmanuel Odogwu. He worked as a bank official. He now lives in New Cross and is a security officer at LSE.

INTERVIEWER Do you have any memories of your time in Nigeria as a young child?

EMMANUEL ODOGWU I was born in Sapele but spent my early teenage years in the Northern part of Nigeria called Kano. My father came to Kano from the South in the fifites. It used to be a very cosmopolitan city. Nobody was conscious whether you are Igbo, Hausa, or Yoruba. I had Hausa friends, I had Yoruba friends, I had Igbo friends but the tribal thing was not there at all. We were just teenage people growing up. That was in the fifties. When Nigeria was still under the British colonial rules. Everything was steady and working very well.

My father was a customs officer. We lived in a privileged custom reserved area for customs officers so we were privileged. Even though we had a priviliged background, we were very free to mix with other local children. I finished my primary and secondary school there.

When we were granted independence in 1960, it was fine. It worked very well at first but then from my memory, that was when tribalism started breeding. Gradually. In a very subtle way, tribalism started growing. They made three tribal groups in Nigeria: the Hausas in the North, the Igbos and the Yorubas in the South. This led to the first political coup in 1966, when the president of Nigeria was assassinated. Because of the riots, the killings were predominently in the North where it was predominantly Hausas, they thought it was the Southerners, the Igbos that started the killings. And so they regrouped, the Hausas regrouped in the North for revenge. That was when the bloodshed started, in 1966.

I remember it was a very very hostile period for everybody. Even for the Northeners but mostly for the Southerners, and especially for the Igbos. The chiefs were calling meetings in their villages and were planning total massacre of the Igbos, especially the Igbos in the North.

I was working for United Bank for Africa. The senior management secretly had a meeting to repatriate all their Southern staff down to the South. They knew what was going to happen. We went to work one day and the manager called us up in his office and explained we had to be repatriated. I remember vividly what happened. We weren't allowed to carry anything. I simply locked up my flat. Our expatriate managers were very careful because they couldn't be seen helping the Southerners. They arranged our flight and drove us down to the airport. I wasn't allowed to carry much. We didn't have an overnight bag so I took a few shirts, a few trousers, rapped it up nicely in a bed sheet and that's what I carried to the airport. I said goodbye to my dad. His office people hid him in his own office. Nobody knew what was happening.

All the Southern bankers were there at Kano airport. A charter plane was arriving. You could see the tension, you could see the soldiers surrounding the perimeters of the airport with their guns. We were all agitated. Where are all these bankers going to? If we allow them to leave, what is going to happen? Are we going to kill them? The plane couldn't carry everyone. I was lucky, I went on the first plane. The plane would touch down at Enugu, capital of the East then. And then come back for a few more. As soon as we were taking off, looking out of the airplane window, I could see the soldiers in the bushes, I could see them with their machine guns. Oh God. And then the plane took off. A few hours later we landed safely at Enugu airport.

INTERVIEWER Did you have any friends who were from Igbo as well, and who were left there? Do you know what happened to them?

EMMANUEL ODOGWU We landed at the airfield there, nowhere to go. We were just refugees. The plan for the plane was to go back to Kano to collect the rest. At about 6 o'clock in the evening, we were in the field, a friend turned up this transistor radio and then we heard from the BBC, of the massacre at Kano airport. They had started shooting those people that were waiting to board the plane before the plane came back. God, I remember, there was hundreds and hundreds that were killed there, in that airport on that particular afternoon. The massacre had started. They were going from house to house, hunting. It was a period of weeks: killing, massacring people in the streets. The image that everybody saw in the South was the image of a headless corpse. The head was missing and the body was put in a trail, and then transported to the South. The image is very vivid.

That were when the bait to Biafra to secede started happening. The authorities in the South decided, that the massacre of the Igbos was the evidence that the Nigerian country did not want the Igbos. The Igbos don't belong to Nigeria. So leaders such as Ojukwu came up.

INTERVIEWER Do you remember him?
EMMANUEL ODOGWU He was a very respected man. He went to a top military school here. He was very respected. And he came from a senior, very rich, privileged background. His father was a very well known politician and a business man in the South. Most of his family assetts went into creating Biafra. We thought Biafra would survive because that's where the oil wealth of Nigeria was. But I am sure that that was why the Nigerian government didn't want Biafra to secede.

INTERVIEWER Can you tell us when the war broke out? How did that then change?
EMMANUEL ODOGWU In Biafra, life was difficult, it was bad. I was lucky again. Working for an international organisation, the bank tried to absorb their staff. But many people were displaced because there was no job. Families were seperated. Refugee camps were springing up from every corner. There were no schools because the schools were used as refugee camps. Nigeria had all the military might. What does Biafra have? Maybe a few, horridly trained to defend their land. They tried but it was tough. All Europe supported Nigeria because they regarded it as internal cessation. They didn't understand the Biafra aspect, the self-determination. They didn't want us in Nigeria so we wanted to govern ourselves. But Nigeria wasn't going to allow it: it is ONE Nigeria.

INTERVIEWER What was your opinion? Did you want one Nigeria?
EMMANUEL ODOGWU That's a very good question. I was for Biafra. I must

admit. I was there in the war. And I was supporting Biafra, because that was what we thought would be a safer place since the other regions didn't want us. Originally I'm from Asaba in Nigeria. Asaba was not part of Biafra then. Asaba was in a Mid-West state. But because we spoke Igbo in that state, we were classified as Igbos.

INTERVIEWER What do you think of the use of propaganda during that time?
EMMANUEL ODOGWU Obviously during wars, everybody wants to put out information to justify what they are doing. Some people blame Ojukwu for taking Biafra to war. But some people were still saying that it was the right thing for Ojukwu to declare Biafra. Propaganda. I would say that during wars, any war at all, propaganda plays a very big role.

INTERVIEWER Were you conscripted?
EMMANUEL ODOGWU No, I wasn't. I didn't want to. I don't have the flair to be a soldier. So I was falling back on my profession as a banker. They gave a list of companies with the essential workers, who are needed for the community. Banks, hospital workers were part of them. They gave us ID cards to show so you wouldn't be conscripted. So for me, that's how I escaped being conscripted: by working in a bank.

Eventually when they still needed more soldiers, they withdrew the special status they gave to the banks. They started recruiting from the banks. So, myself and a few friends, we founded a dramatic society. And we decided that we would go to the military hospitals to entertain the wounded soldiers with drama.

I remember the first play we acted. It was a Ghanain author. We got a few sponsors that gave us a van and a few things for costumes. And we took this play on the road. So we got some of the military officers to recognise us as essential for the wounded soldiers. And we were given the ID cards to carry around so nobody would conscript us. We were taken to military hospitals and performed to wounded soldiers. They would give us a big hall, we would put on this show, spend the night there in the camp and go back. That was our way: we acted and this continued straight through the end of the war.

It's amazing what you can develop during the war: the talents you don't know you have. During the war, you would do anything to survive.

INTERVIEWER So do you think that putting on this play brought a smile to the soldiers?

EMMANUEL ODOGWU There's no question about that. Yes. That's one of the satisfactions I got from it. Even though it kept me out of the army, out of being a soldier, it also gave me this satisfaction. After acting, you could see people on crutches, wounded soldiers with bandages in the front row, you could see them with their smiles, applauding you.

INTERVIEWER What kind of play was it? Were they British or traditional African plays?

EMMANUEL ODOGWU It was a traditional African play. It was *"The dilemma of a Ghost"* by Ama Ata Aidoo. The plot is this African went to somewhere in Europe, got married to a white girl and brought her back to the village, and everything that Africans were doing was strange for her. It was funny. It was good. I remember that very well. It was the English culture trying to mix with the African culture. It was a very popular one. We took it around to different hospitals, different towns. We didn't get paid. We were lucky if they gave us some allowances. But most of us were still working. I was still working in the bank. It lasted until the end of the war.

The way the Biafran war was happening: when a town fell to Nigeria, everybody disorganised, you moved on to another place until the next one: from Port Harcourt, I moved down to Owerri, from Owerri I moved down to Aba, from Aba, I moved to Ehala. Different areas. That's how the whole thing disintergrates, how communities break up. So when one town falls, it takes a while to find the others. It's dreadful. In fact when refugees were carrying their little possessions escaping, the air raid was still coming down.

INTERVIEWER What happened to your family left back in Kano?

EMMANUEL ODOGWU The majority of my family were from Asaba. After the Kano massacre, the majority of my parents came out to Biafra. We were very lucky. Even my grandfather in his old age was able to cross over on foot, on foot, to come to our place. So those that were left behind, were my father and two of my brothers, left in Kano. Negotiations for a ceasefire was agreed and everybody who was in hiding, was allowed to come out. And they had to organise evacuations back to the South. So that was when my father came back to the South.

INTERVIEWER What was the atmosphere like when the war ended?

EMMANUEL ODOGWU The atmosphere was jubilation. The end of the suffering: jubilation. I was a bachelor then, when the war ended. I didn't know. Some guy just came to the village and said "the war ended" and I

Above: Graduation of Nikki, London, 2004;
Centre: Hosting christmas party for staff children, Abba, 1974
Below left: Emmanuel at work, Onitsha, 1972; Right: Wedding day, Benin city, 1973

said "what are you talking about?". He said "Go up to the high street, you will see Nigerian soldiers and Biafran soldiers, everybody jubilating". I went down and "Oh yes the war has ended".

The question then was how do you make your way back home? Who's going to give you money for transportation? The Biafran currency we were carrying was worthless. Worthless. But in that atmosphere, everybody wants to be everybody's helper. You could just drop into a vehicle going your way. As long as the driver had room to carry you, they would take you to the place where you can change. It took me about a day or so, a whole day of travelling to go back to Asaba.

INTERVIEWER So there wasn't a feeling of being defeated?
EMMANUEL ODOGWU To some. But to the majority, no. It came to a point that there wasn't a feeling of being defeated. All the Biafran leaders had all gone. Ojukwu went away. All the military people who were at the head of the country had all gone. They had all escaped. Some of them were captured. Maybe by ceasefire agreement, they were given an easy passage.

INTERVIEWER How did that make you feel, that Ojukwu left?
EMMANUEL ODOGWU He gave it a try. He gave it a shot. He had a lot of sympathy. In fact until now, that is why he's still popular. Until now, people still regard him highly that he gave his best shot. His personal assetts, his personal fortune went into the war. Because of his popularity, when he came back and went into politics he represented the Igbos. That is why he is still popular.

INTERVIEWER When and why did you leave to go to London?
EMMANUEL ODOGWU After the war in1970, it was a new start for everybody in Biafra. People who came from Biafra were about five years backwards because in Biafra, during the war, schools shut down, economy shut down. So in 1970, it was a new beginning for us. I was lucky again. The bank absorbed us into Nigeria. I started working and everything was back to normal again. I began to enjoy the good things of life. I got married.

But personally for me, there came a point where I wanted adventure, I wanted to move ashore. I had never been to Europe before. I wanted to go to Europe. I wanted to follow my education. I was already married then with a son, Henry.

INTERVIEWER What things did you hear about Britain? What made you want to come?

EMMANUEL ODOGWU I had friends and relations already here but the mentality we had at that time was "when you are in Europe, everything is easy". But at my mature age then, I didn't think that. I came here first alone. I got a bedsit in Tulse Hill owned by an Irish guy. In Nigeria I had a big garden, a big house. And I came down here and had a little bedsit.

I registered in a school of banking in 1979. I came to this country in January 1979 during a big winter. And one week later, I was at school. A banker a few months ago. Now, a student.

I was communicating with my wife. I said to my wife "Look, I'm coming in the summer to take you guys. I'm not complete without you guys". So I left here in July, I just had my exams, good papers came out. And then I travelled to where my family was, in Aba. I made sure they were ready to come with me. I came back on my own and then they joined me a few months later. And that was the same year, in 1979.

INTERVIEWER How did you find the cultural difference?

EMMANUEL ODOGWU That was really tough. Initially, when my wife and my child came to join me, we stayed in the same bedsit. Poor Henry. He had no place to play. I bought him some toys. But he was knocking his head all over. It was a cramped room. Eventually we progressed. We progressed a little bit. Two rooms became vacant in the same house. So I asked my Irish landlord. He was very good although he increased the rent obviously.

As a student, I wasn't allowed to work, it was a restriction as students. You are supposed to be having funds from your sponsors to pay your fees. But we had nobody sponsoring us. So all the work we were doing was black market work. Hiding and working. My wife got a job in a supermarket as a cashier. She was only in the country for 8 weeks. From Africa, from Nigeria! And already she had a job and with a currency she never had seen before. But we were determined to succeed.

I would go to this big agency. They have a place somewhere in Liverpool Street. For you to get a job, you have to be there by 5 o'clock in the morning. They were specialised in catering. That was a very popular job with Nigerian students then. And if you are really lucky, you get a security guard job. As a student you want a security job because you go there, you sit down there and carry on with your textbooks. But people would sleep sleepless nights. You would come out of work in the morning and then you would go to college. Straight from work to college. But that's how most of us survived.

INTERVIEWER After you graduated, did you move into a job?

Emmanuel Odogwu's family in 1997 during a family visit to newly buit house in Asaba, Nigeria - From top to bottom: Henry, Niki, Chuka and Heanyi, Emmanuel, Gladys

EMMANUEL ODOGWU For ten years I had been applying for visas as a student. And then, after ten years, I decided I was tired of these student visa applications. I decided having been a good citizen, a good student, I didn't have any problems, I've been living in the country for ten years, my young child was growing up here, I had a second child... so I decided to apply for Indefinite Leave to Remain. I didn't have money to consult any legal advisors so I collected all the information myself. I brought out all my certificates that I had acquired. All my qualifications. I got recommendations from local communities, my church, some friends and then I applied. When I told my friends I was applying, they were a bit sceptical. If they refuse us, that's the end of it. It's deportation. But it came to a point where if we are asked to go, then let's go. I went to Lunar House in Croydon and submitted my application. The guy looked at it, stamped a receipt and gave it to me. And then I went back, they told me it normally takes about six months to twelve months to get a reply.

But one day, as I was indoors, the post man knocked at the door and I received a brown enveloppe from Her Majesty's Service. That was barely three weeks after. I said "My God, this is good. This is really great." I opened the envelope. I found three passports: Henry's passport, my wife's passport and my own Nigerian passport. And then, the first letter I opened was my own: "The Secretary of State is pleased to grant you Indefinite Leave to Remain." I read it again: "The Secretary of State is pleased to grant you Indefinite Leave to Remain." I read my wife's letter: same thing. I read my Son's one: same thing. It was a great relief. Now you can plan your life. Now you can be free. You can go and look for proper jobs.

I still felt Nigerian. A Nigerian given Leave to Remain in the country. I still had my Nigerian passport. But now I can move. I can travel without coming back and asking for a visa.

INTERVIEWER When did you feel that you were British?
EMMANUEL ODOGWU At the time, the Nigerian government did not allow the citizens to have dual citizenship. So if you wanted to apply to be a British citizen, you had to surrender your nationality, your Nigerian passport. Few people did that. I didn't want to. So I was amongst those who were lobbying the Nigerian government, that it is to our own interest, to our country's interest to allow your citizens in the UK who have Indifinite Leave to Remain, to apply for citizenship, and still be Nigerian citizens. Luckily after two years, they approved. When the Nigerian government approved, it was hailed as a big success for the lobbying group here. Now I was able to apply. Meanwhile, I was working, I was paying my taxes. That

was one of the conditions they wanted: Are you working? Are you paying your taxes? Are you going to rely on state funds? I have never relied on state funds. I have never claimed a penny. I don't have any file at all at the dole office. So I was quite positive when I applied. I got my friends recommendations again. Because you have to be recommended by British citizens.

INTERVIEWER Why did you think it was important for you to maintain both the heritages?
EMMANUEL ODOGWU First, I'm a Nigerian. I didnt want to lose that identity at all. But to get a British citizenship, it was getting the best of both worlds: Best of British, best of Nigeria. I didn't want to lose that Nigerian identity. I wanted to keep it. It was very important. That was my background. That's what made me who I am. When you travel out, you learn cultures, you enrich your background, you enrich your foundations, what you already have. So many good things were picked up here: the discipline, the self-respect, the self-esteem.

INTERVIEWER So, would you go back to Nigeria to live?
EMMANUEL ODOGWU I dont think so because now it is a privileged position to have two homes. Not everybody has two places you call home. This is home. I go back to Nigeria today, I have a home. Rather than pack up completely to go to Nigeria to live, I would be living in both places. During the winter months, when you are all putting your heating, your blankets, I would just leave here and go to sunshine Africa, put on my t-shirt, slippers and sandals and in the summer I would come back here. So I would enjoy the best of both worlds. But I don't think there would be a time where I would pack my bags and go. No. It has come to a stage now: I have lived in this country for over 30 years now. It is not something you can just throw behind you like it never existed.

INTERVIEWER How did you raise your children? Did you raise them as British or Nigerian? Did you speak your language to them at home?
EMMANUEL ODOGWU I must admit: no. That is where we failed as parents. Yes I won't hesitate to admit that fault. We joined the people that made that mistake of speaking English to their children at home. We came here we thought that speaking English to your children would make them what they are. When we realised the mistake, we started correcting. I wouldnt say it was late. But better late than never. So I started speaking Igbo to them. Most of them picked up. They cannot respond but at least they begin to

understand. We wanted to make sure they have this identity that they are Nigerians. That's why we take them home, take them on holidays, so that Henry can survive well in Nigeria, in Asaba. And here as well.

INTERVIEWER What would your children identify themselves as?
EMMANUEL ODOGWU When, I fill forms, I write I am British. I don't call myself Nigerian here. I call myself British. We have two passports. They both have a British passport and a Nigerian passport.

INTERVIEWER What do they feel in their heart?
EMMANUEL ODOGWU I would think here. I would think they feel more British than Nigerians. Because this is the culture they grew up in. And two, three weeks holidays in Nigeria won't make them Nigerians. They don't know the culture. They are beginning to understand the culture. But they didnt grow up there. They didn't go to school there.

Everything I told you, they know it because they know the history, they know how we came here. As they say, they admire Mom and Dad, for being that humble, and bringing them here. And sometimes they thank us for the good life we've given them, for that decision. I tell them that maybe you would have had the same opportunity if we were back home, we would have tried to give you the same life. I think, to them, the belief is that they are British. Yes, they think they are British.

INTERVIEWER What is your aspiration for the future of Nigeria?
EMMANUEL ODOGWU Nigeria. My aspiration. If you asked me many years ago, it was very gloom. I didn't know what was happening in that country with all the military, the rules, the politicians, the corruption. But I can see some light now. I can see a few good things coming out now. I don't know if you are aware, they have just concluded an election which has been regarded as a very fair election, that brought for the first time a very undisputed leader to the country. So I'm just hoping that Nigeria will build on this success and provide a good future for the next generations to come.

FOOD FOR THOUGHT
Do you agree with Emmanuel Odogwu that it is important for the children to know both their heritages?

In what ways can you relate to Emmanuel's story?

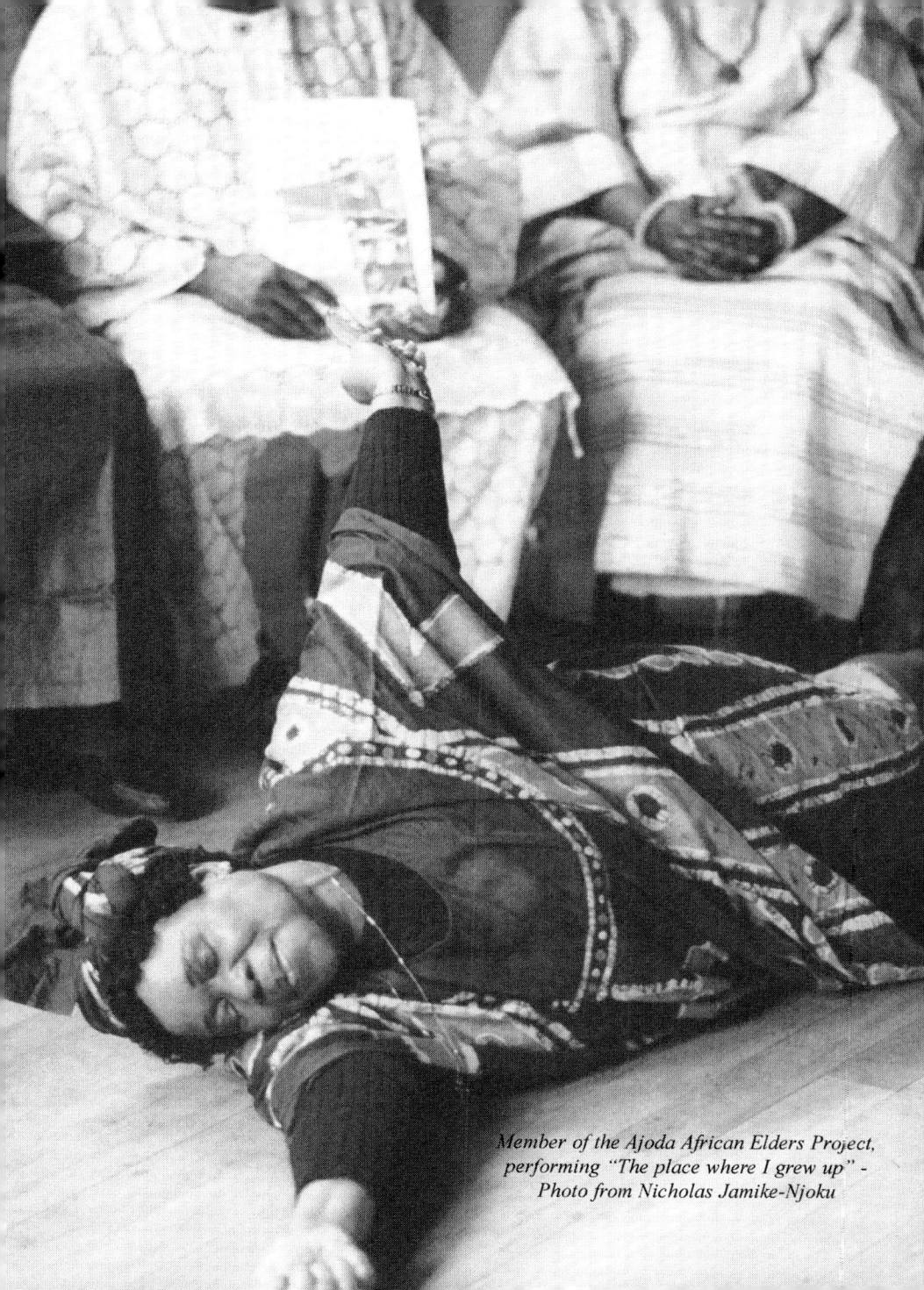

Member of the Ajoda African Elders Project, performing "The place where I grew up" - Photo from Nicholas Jamike-Njoku

INTERVIEW WITH NICHOLAS JAMIKE-NJOKU

Nicholas Jamike-Njoku was born the 25th of December, 1938 in Imo, part of Eastern Nigeria. He then moved to Lagos where he attended secondary school and university before coming to the UK in 1965 on a Federal government scholarship. He runs the Ajoda African Elderly project in Woolwich.

INTERVIEWER Since the war, did you stay in the UK or did you go back?
NICHOLAS JAMIKE The war was a very sad experience. The war is an ill wind that blows nobody good. Both the victor and the defeated are the same. My experiences of the war goes from the start of the war to the end of it. I was in Nigeria knowing what was going on within the military. We knew the country was very shaky. There was a bit of turbulence in the army, as it is now in Nigeria, anything could happen at any moment. The army had many Northerners but was predominantly governed or ruled by the South-Easterners or the South, they were the officers, the elite or the intellectuals in the army in those days. So the core of the war, I am aware is because of the pogrom that started in the North, in those days to drive away the Southerners from the North but unfortunately the pogrom was subjected only to the people of the Eastern part of the country which was the Igbos. By far, I should identify myself here as a Biafran. But the war has ended, we have regrouped and we can still call ourselves Nigerians.

INTERVIEWER When you moved over here, did you start studying or were you working?
NICHOLAS JAMIKE I studied here for years, got my degrees. I worked very, very well. During the war, I had three jobs. To meet the cost of the war – the Biafran side was not prepared for the war, so the armament and the ammunitions were not there. We had no fire jets, we had no war planes, nor did we have armory, so all we did here was to work very hard, so that we could support them back home. When you talk about war, we are not fighting Nigeria per se, we are fighting the whole global war, Britain here, America, Russia were in support of the war, even France who promised Biafra that they were going to recognise them, they were also part of the armament delivery to the Nigerian side of the war.

However, when I was here, I maintained about three jobs. Which means that you go to work round the clock. Some of us paid about three thousand or four thousand to the Biafran common fund, to prosecute the war. I was a hospital engineer at Kings College hospital. In fact they themselves supported my training here, I am gifted perhaps, I had the Kings fund.

INTERVIEWER Did you hear any stories of your family back home?
NICHOLAS JAMIKE During the time of the war, you couldn't hear of anything from home, except disasters all the time because you cannot even pinpoint where your family is. When I got back to Nigeria, I couldn't identify our house, they riddled things down and all that. These are some sad experiences, which I dare not wish on anybody.

INTERVIEWER When you moved over here, did you go back at any point and come back again?
NICHOLAS JAMIKE No, since the war, I lost my identity as a Nigerian. In fact I threw away my passport and went to the British to get another passport, and that same day I got citizenship. It was as bad as that.

After a while, in 1978, I went back to Nigeria. By that time things had really cooled down, and according to those leaders those days, they said there is no victory, no vanquished.

INTERVIEWER Would you say you are British or Nigerian?
NICHOLAS JAMIKE Well as a matter of fact, I should still say that I am both, because I worked in Nigeria. I left the UK in 1978, went to Nigeria, worked as a lecturer and bio medical engineer, and also as a national coordinator of all the universities of bio medical engineering in Nigeria, as well as a

Members of the Ajoda African Elders project performing "The place where I grew up"

consultant to the petroleum trust fund, on bio medical equipment. So I can say really that I have enjoyed both Nigeria and here. Now that I have retired in Nigeria, I am retired here too. At least I have seen both sides of the coin, and I love to be here as I am today because it is more peaceful.

INTERVIEWER About your children living and raising them in England, what do you consider them?

NICHOLAS JAMIKE I took my children to Nigeria. They all got their education in Nigeria, and got their post here, so they have seen part of where we come from, they can identify themselves to our roots, where we have aunts, uncles and relations. Some of them are back here, some of them are still in Nigeria.

Nicholas Jamike when he first arrived in London

INTERVIEWER What would you like Nigeria's legacy to be?

NICHOLAS JAMIKE It is a very big question. Nigeria's legacy should be that of a country which all should call our own, irrespective of creed, tribe, ethnic connections, irrespective of where you come from. These are the things I really desire as a legacy for Nigeria.

FOOD FOR THOUGHT
What can each of us do to prevent our communities and the rest of the world from falling deeper into the cycle of violence and revenge?

Right: Member of the Ajoda African Elders project performing "The place where I grew up"

Interview with Margaret Ilide

Margaret Ilide was born on the 16th of October, 1936 in a town named Wamba, Nigeria. Her father worked for the colonier masters in the mines of Wamba. She lives in Ushie Delta State and is retired.

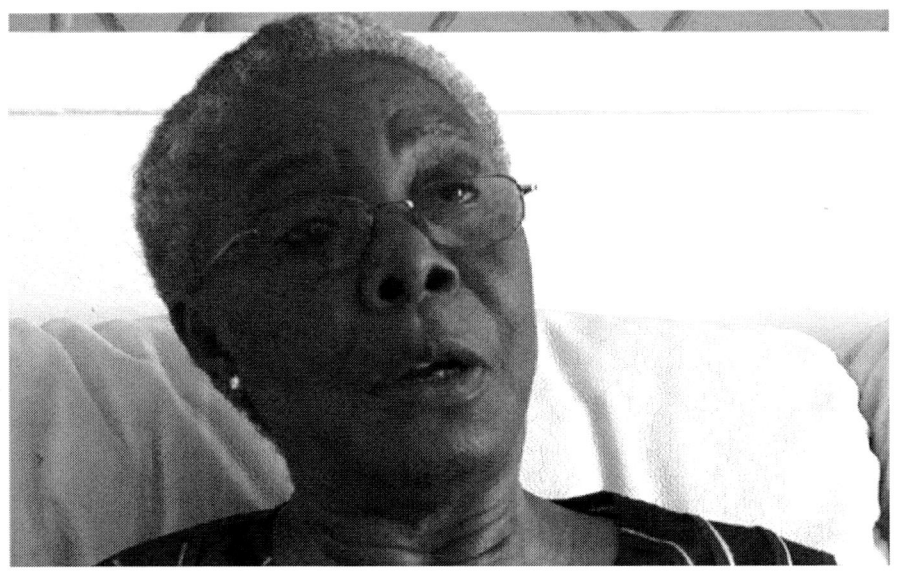

Interviewer Could you go through your early experiences of being a child in Nigeria?
Margaret Ilide In Wamba I went to a private school for Standard One from 1944 to 1948. Wamba was a small camp, the school there ended in Standard One so I had to go back to Jos to live with my father's landlady in Jos, and there I completed my Standard Six. After the completion of my school, my father decided to resign and go back to the village, so we went back to the village in 1952.

Interviewer When did you come to this country and what were your first experiences here?
Margaret Ilide I got married in Lagos to Mr Obi Fred Ilide when I was 16 years old. We lived in Lagos from 1952 to 1958. My husband Fred Obi

Ilide worked as a clerk in a shipping company called Palm Line Agency in Apapa. He resigned his work in 1959 and then prepared to come down to London to study in August 1960. Two years later I joined him. I was here in London from 1962 to 1965. I went to the school of dress making as a designer in Shoreditch College of Dressing Industry. I finished my course in 1964. Then I was pregnant. From early 1964 to late 1964, my husband had to send me back to Nigeria to go and have the baby, we couldn't afford to have a baby here in London because we were all students. So they had to send me back home to have the baby, and after having the baby, I had to drop the baby to our parents and come back to join my husband until he finished his education, and then we would come back together. But unfortunately when I went to have my baby, the war started. I had that child in September 1965. When the war started in 1966, the baby was five months old.

INTERVIEWER You said you were here in the 1960's, can you describe your first time being here? What were the communities like when you first arrived here?

MARGARET ILIDE When I first came here, London was a dark city; things were not as normal as it is now. Winter was so severe, we normally had the winter warmer, called the Paraffin Winter Warmer, we use it with paraffin just like a stove and by that time things were very normal.

The English ones were so friendly, we lived with them like students. The economy at that time was very good because we used the same Pound Sterling until Nigeria changed to Naira.

Before you come to Great Britain, you have to register for a school where you study and then you have to have enough money to keep up your studies, so when my husband came down to London he came down to London with £3000 to continue his education. By the time I joined him, he took me to a full time course. We were both students during our time and things were so good.

INTERVIEWER Were Black and Whites living equally?

MARGARET ILIDE Yes, of course we were living equally. When we were here we had the opportunities of buying houses, and we paid the way you people pay now. Some people pay for ten years then that becomes a mortgage, my husband bought a house in 83 Rodding Road. So by the time I left, my husband had paid all his mortgage and that house belonged to him, he lived equally with the whites and there was no discrimination at all.

INTERVIEWER When you went back to Nigeria, you said that the war had started. What was it like?
MARGARET ILIDE My baby was five months old when the war started. There was a coup in Nigeria. In Nigeria at the time, there was four regions: the North, the West, the East and the Mid-West. Our own place was in the Mid-West. When the coup started in January 1967, the prime ministers from the four regions were assassinated and the army took over. The brigade chief that took over was Aguiyi-Ironsi. After six months when he was going for a meeting in the North, he was assassinated in Ikeja Airport. Then after his assassination, all the prime ministers were killed, leaving the only one who was from the Eastern region. He ran for exile, Okpara ran

Left: Catherine Enyabine (stepmother), Tokunbo Ilide (daughter) Theresa Ilide-Francis (mother) Catherine Ilide (daughter), Margaret Ilide
Right: Theresa Ilide and Jennifer Maleghemi (daughter) at Green Park London in the 80s.

away during the coup, but the Northern prime minister and the Western prime minister were assassinated with the governors.

INTERVIEWER What were your experiences like when you got there during the war?
MARGARET ILIDE Ojukwu came to Lagos to meet with the council of elders, after meeting with the councils of elders, Ojukwu went back to the East and declared Biafra. He said that they would not belong to Nigeria anymore, that they are Biafrans. After declaring Biafra, Ojukwu announced on the radio that all the Igbos should come back to the East. So we started migrating from Lagos. All the Igbos migrated to their places in the East. People from the Mid-West had to send their families back home, send their wives back home. Even my dad and his brothers were there in Lagos. When the war started, we were in the village, but we didn't even know that that place would become a war front, that we are going for safety.

INTERVIEWER Can you describe your personal experience during the war?
MARGARET ILIDE During the war, it was terrible, there was a river from Onitsha which is the East and it follows on to our place, from Abor to Ashaka and to Umusadege. So from that creek, the Biafran and Nigerian armies started warring each other.

We could hear shelling because it was nine miles away from my village. During a certain time the Biafrans were short of their warring bullets, so they decided to make local guns. They plant them in the farms with wire, with some pieces of broken glasses, they connect it and one person would climb up. By the time the Nigerian troops would cross that creek to the other side, they would trigger the gun and all the people would be killed. They used that to destroy so many Nigerian armies.

When my children would go to the river bank - because we don't have a water pipe, we normally drink and wash our clothes at the river - they would run back that they are bringing some troops, Nigerian troops killed at the war front. We saw a lot of armies being killed those days.

When they would come for an attack, we would flee. At times we would flee to the bush and sometimes we were so scared. Sometimes we wouldn't put something at the top of the table because when they start shelling, the echo would be shaking our houses and things would be dropping. It was so terrible.

INTERVIEWER What happened at the end of the war?
MARGARET ILIDE At that particular time, the Biafrans were short of salt

and corn. When they were short of those things, we from the Mid-West started sending those things through the creek. But the army would catch some of us trying to smuggle those things to them, they would shoot them. They would ask them to dig their own graves and when they dug their graves they would shoot them inside and bury them. That was a terrible experience and if they didn't want to kill them, they would ask them to lie down and face the sun for about four or five hours. They really killed a lot of our people because of helping the Biafrans to survive during the war.

INTERVIEWER During the war, were you lacking in any way?
MARGARET ILIDE We did not lack of anything, because we were on the Nigerian side. It got to a point where the Biafrans took over the Mid-West but after some time the Nigerian army troops took back the Delta area. That day, they killed so many people in Asaba: 1000 men were massacred in Asaba. And when they crossed back to Onitsha, they blew up the bridge. So there was no link between them and us.

They also raped women and even in the presence of their husbands. When the husband resisted, they would shoot them. I did not have that experience of raping because my husband's people were around, so when they came to me I reported them, so they caught them and gave them punishment. They would come with force, they said their Head of the Brigade wants to see me but I told them that I have a husband, they have no right to see me. They said they will force me to go, they were speaking the Hausa language and I understand Hausa language. As they were speaking I answered to them that I am not going to go there, that I am married and that they should go and tell their brigade or whatever his name is that I am not going to go with them. When they heard that I understood their language, they had to leave me alone.

INTERVIEWER After the war, people heard that Ojukwu left, what was the atmosphere like?
MARGARET ILIDE The very day the Biafrans surrendered, everybody was so happy. People started coming back. I had two brothers in Port Harcourt, as I was just sitting down one day, I noticed that my brother had come down from Biafra, so I went to the lieutenant - the name of the lieutenant was lieutenant Mike - and I said he had to release my brother to me, and we were very happy.

INTERVIEWER At the time, it was Biafrans against Nigerians what did you see yourself as? Did you see yourself as a Nigerian or a Biafran?

MARGARET ILIDE We speak almost the same language as the Igbos, we speak "Bia" so they said that all the people that are speaking Bia are Biafrans. So when the Nigerian troops came in to take back the Mid-West they nearly wanted to kill us. They actually came and killed some of our people in Warri market, but after some time they came to know that we are not from the East so we were left alone.

Margaret Ilide (Trafalgar square in the 1990s, on holiday)

Interviewer Was all your family in the East or were they in Lagos?
Margaret Ilide My daddy and all my other brothers were in Lagos, but me, my mother, my children and other of my relations were in the village so after the war we had to return back to Lagos.

Interviewer What did you think about Biafra? Did you think that Ojukwu was right to start the war?
Margaret Ilide Nobody will say that war is right. War is bloody, nobody knew that the war would go to that extent of division.

Interviewer What do you think of Nigeria now in the 21st century, do you think that it has developed since the war?
Margaret Ilide Before, Nigerians didn't know how to pull a trigger, or use a gun but after the war, armed robberies started, young ones knew how to use a gun. Some of them hid guns in their homes. After the war, things were very hard and we started seeing these armed robberies. Before we didn't have much armed robbery. So this war brought what they call Western civilisation, to use guns to rob.

Nigeria has developed a lot, changes have been made since our own time. We didn't have many educated people but now Nigeria has many educated people. We have more universities, things have changed.

Interviewer What would be your message to children growing up now in the Diaspora?
Margaret Ilide After the war, when things were not going right people started going into Britain and America to seek for green pastures. But now that Nigeria has changed, we ask our people to go back, and build a new Nigeria, that will be profitable for our children in the future, and so that we will not remain here looking for green pastures.

> **FOOD FOR THOUGHT**
> Respect comes from understanding, but misunderstanding leads to disrespect. How can we build lives based on respect for one another?

INTERVIEW WITH DR OSITA OKAGBUE

Dr Osita Okagbue was born on the 29th of May, 1954 in Onitsha, South East Nigeria. He came to the UK in 1986 on a Commonwealth scholarship to study at Leeds University. He completed his PhD in Plymouth in 2001 and is now a lecturer at Goldsmiths College, University of London.

INTERVIEWER Was your school quite multicultural in Onitsha?
DR OSITA OKAGBUE I attended St John's primary school briefly in Onitsha, but it was only in Umuahia that I for the first time met people from other ethnic groups. We had two or three Hausa boys in our class. When the pogrom started, one of the first things we noticed is that we didn't see them again, they had gone. We all used to go out riding bikes on the street. In Onitsha it wasn't multicultural or mutli-ethinic or maybe I didn't notice it, but in Umuahia it was more significant. We all used to go out and play on the streets and we were fascinated by their names and the fact that they could speak Igbo like us. We fitted quite well, we didn't see them as different. We just knew that they ate different kinds of food, had another language that we didn't speak. Apart from that they were pretty much like every other person. There was no prejudice at all.

INTERVIEWER Where were you in 1966 before the breakout of the war?
DR OSITA OKAGBUE In 1966, I was still in high school in the first year so yes, I remember the military coup and that a lot of people celebrated the military coup in the Eastern region. We had the perception that politics wasn't going right and that the elected politicians were not doing the right thing. So when the military came, there was a sense of optimism.

INTERVIEWER Do you remember the killings that happened in the North?
DR OSITA OKAGBUE I can't say I remember but I was aware, I saw people who were streaming back. I didn't loose anybody in my own family but I knew people who lost people. So to that extent it was pretty much obvious what was happening. And of course there were the images in the newspaper and the tales that people told when they came back. And because Umuahia was along the railway line, there were streams of trains coming in and bringing people from the North. We were able to see those as well because we lived in a railway town.

When the war broke out, I was in secondary school, and we carried on until schools broke up in 1967 and then we were all sent home. There wasn't any attempt for education then. We just hung around. A lot of us wanted to join the army. But I wasn't old enough, they chased us away and said we were too young. Some of us were caught in between: we were too young to join the army and too old to be in the boys company. The boys company was for the younger chaps and so we were caught in between. But I joined the Red Cross.

INTERVIEWER Can you tell us about your work with the Red Cross?
DR OSITA OKAGBUE The Red Cross was a very good experience for me, we used to just sit in the office, people would come in and we would dispense painkillers and stuff like that. And we were trained on how to dress wounds, but between late 1968 and 1969 we were actually taken to the war front a few times and that was quite an eye opener.

We saw soldiers going into battle: some of them coming out injured, some of them coming out dead. If the Biafran army advanced, we moved with them and if they retreated, we retreated with them. It made me grow up, seeing soldiers you had shared discussions with some weeks before, and now coming out on stretchers, either dead or injured and then having to treat them.

I must have been about fifteen. Sometimes you were asked to go dig the trenches for the soldiers. We were very keen to contribute. At some point, we started feeling more comfortable in the warfront than at home. And that was ironic, in the sense that everybody thought that you were facing more danger in the front. So I found myself asking the Red Cross if there were any operations to go to the warfront, we felt safer there because we had our bunkers where we treated the soldiers. One of the reasons why we felt more comfortable in staying there is that each time there was an operation, and Biafra gained ground my town was rocketed and shelled quite a lot and people died. But the shells and the rockets went above the heads of the soldiers in the front so if you were up there all you had to fear were bullets. While at home you had sniper bullets that travel quite a distance, and rockets and grenades that can come and destroy houses, kill people. So at home, every family had a bunker that you ran into when the shells took off. But not everybody managed to make it to the bunkers before the shells arrived.

INTERVIEWER Did you support Ojukwu, did you agree?
DR OSITA OKAGBUE Yes, wholeheartedly, yes. As I said at the beginning, when the military coup took place, a lot of people felt that the politicians were corrupt, whether they were Igbo, Hausa or Yoruba politicians. They weren't doing the right thing and so people felt disappointed and disillusioned with independence. The freedom that people hoped for, the better life that people hoped for never came. So when Nzeogwu and five Majors carried out the coup everybody thought this was good, its going to stop the drift in politics and institute a new system of governance, which will maybe help to achieve the dreams of independence.

Aguiyi-Ironsi then became the Head of State, an Igbo man. I think that was the mistake that the coup plotters made. Because they did not kill Ironsi, they were perceived to be very biased in the way they executed the coup. I think that was one of the grave mistakes they made and secondly, the fact that they did not kill the Premier of Eastern region Dr Michael Okpara, who was lucky that he had a visitor. I think he was being visited by Archbishop Makarios of Cyprus at the time so they didn't go into killing him; they waited. The perception was that the coup was flawed and biased in favour of Igbo politicians.

When the second coup happened and Aguiyi-Ironsi was killed and Gowon took over, everyone thought why should it be Gowon, he wasn't the highest ranking, he was a Lieutenant Colonel, even though Aguiyi-Ironsi brought him back and made him chief of staff.

So to answer your question, everybody that I know in the East supported Biafra, even with the way the government was run and eventually there were cracks everybody started seeing, also flaws in Ojukwu himself.

INTERVIEWER What about the use of propaganda at the time?
DR OSITA OKAGBUE I think the Biafra propaganda machine was quite effective. There was one particular radio broadcaster called Okoko Ndem. He was quite effective. I remember when Gowon visited the East after the war, he wanted to meet Okoko Ndem. We weren't outside Biafra so we wouldn't know, but as far as we were concerned the way the war was presented to us. There were lies, when major cities fell, you weren't told immediately, but of course gradually, everybody knew that things weren't going right. But I cannot say for sure whether people really thought of surrendering, it came as a surprise. It was a surprise contained with relief, because at the end of the day, people didn't know if they were prepared to all die in pursuit of Biafra.

INTERVIEWER How did you feel when Ojukwu left?
DR OSITA OKAGBUE He had to go because there was no other way. They would have killed him, so he had to go. It was almost like there was a personal battle between him and Gowon. And Ojukwu was a bit arrogant. Ojukwu comes from a very privileged family. His father was a millionaire at that time, there weren't so many in Nigeria then and to have gone to Oxford, he lived a privileged life. Ojukwu came from very solid money and that translated into his attitude a lot. He used to think he was better than all the military, including the Head of State, then Major General Aguiyi-Ironsi.

INTERVIEWER What was the British interest in Nigeria at that time?
DR OSITA OKAGBUE Britain created part of the problem, didn't they? Britain put together a group of very strong-minded national groups and formed them into a country in 1914 - because it was administratively fine under colonialism to put them together. But to do that without putting in place structures that will manage it properly, that was the mistake Britain made. They made promises to the North because the Yorubas, the Igbos and a few other people in the South wanted to have independence before 1960, but the North said they weren't ready. People felt they were always supporting the North because it was easier to rule in the North. Indirect rule worked much better in the North than it did in the South, especially in the Igbo speaking areas. In the North, all you needed to do was to get the leader sign a treaty but in the South, especially in the Igboland, they had to sign individual treaties with little villages and towns.

The Igbos have had cities, states that operated in a kind of democratic system, they had the age grades and then they appointed a leader, a spokesperson. But you don't have extra privileges because you are a king, you don't control people's lives. If the village or the town needed to be represented outside, you did that, and in exchange people worked for you. They would donate labour to you on your farm, they would help build your house. That was the kind of leadership that the Igbos had.

The British tried to change that because they needed a firm leader. But the leader didn't bring people along all the time. You always heard them screaming and protesting, so I believe that the British had difficulties dealing with the Igbos.

INTERVIEWER Can you talk about the poets and artists during that period?
DR OSITA OKAGBUE One of the things I remember very well was that the Biafra government tried to use the artists quite a lot. I remember the playwright Sonny Oti, he is dead now but he wrote plays and he was a wonderful composer. I remember one of the songs called the *"Biafran Child"*. They used to have the Biafran choral group that used to sing on television and radio, singing about the war, composing war songs for the soldiers and a lot of people. The arts were quite well respected by the government and that's why a lot of these artists, Chinua Achebe, Obiechina and others were drafted in as advisors to the government. That is why they had a very effective propaganda machine, they had people who had ability with words, who could use words to make a point. Okoko Ndem who was from the cross river state, he had a wonderful voice, but he had things scripted.

INTERVIEWER What about Okigbo? What kind of work did he do?
DR OSITA OKAGBUE He was the first African poet that really had an effect on me. When I sat the entrance exam to the university, it was his poem that I used. Christopher Okigbo was a soldier in the Biafran army but he died in the war front. I read his poems, I think it was a collection called *"Path of Thunder"* and the first poem there is *"Heavensgate"*. One of the lines is "Under your power wait I on barefoot, watchman for the watchword at Heavensgate". That poem resonated with me. Okigbo's poetry was quite complex and his collection showed me that you can naturally follow a poet as a kind of journey. In *"Path of Thunder"*, he created different landscapes and it's only as you read, and by knowing the symbolism and the metaphors that he uses, that you begin to associate a lot of them with actual happenings within the country. The poems were formed in such a way that you were taken through this wonderful landscape. You find the trees and the vegetation that you are very familiar with, where you grew up. There is always an element of water, of the stream, of nature.

INTERVIEWER Do you think his poetry brought peace to some of the soldiers?

DR OSITA OKAGBUE I don't know whether the soldiers read the poems, he wrote a lot of the poems before he went to war. I don't know how many he wrote as a soldier but you could see in the poems that he was already grappling with the politics of the situation. He says he writes his poems for poets but he was somebody with a very sensitive soul, and of course with all the other people around him, he was one of the few who went to join the army and died. He was a typical artist, he felt more than other people.

INTERVIEWER What about Wole Soyinka's work at that time?

DR OSITA OKAGBUE I didn't know a lot about Wole Soyinka's work. The only few African artists I knew at the time were people like Chinua Achebe. We became aware of Wole Soyinka because we heard that this very famous writer, a Yoruba person had come to Enugu, to meet with Ojukwu, to persuade him not to take Biafra out of the republic. And that then he went to prison for it. I felt that he must be a very important person because the students at Ibadan University were always talking about him, and so I knew he must be somebody. We then heard that he staged his one-man takeover at the radio station in the West. He was that kind of person. You could see a similarity between him and Okigbo, they were artists who not only tried to address the issue in their work but were also prepared to actually be politically engaged in the situation: Soyinka in dialogue with the politicians was telling them what he thought was wrong with what they were doing; and Okigbo by taking up arms to defend.

INTERVIEWER What about Chinua Achebe at that time?

DR OSITA OKAGBUE I think he was the one at that time running Biafran information service, because he was already working in the Nigerian information service, so he transferred into the Biafran one. So you may call them the ideas people behind Biafra, and a lot of times they were making connections, they were sent out on international visits to preach and to plead the Biafran cause to governments. There was a general feeling among Igbo people that Biafra was right because there was no other way.

I think part of our problem is that the leadership has never bothered to harness all of our resources together. That is the sad thing: the human resources are there, the mineral resources are there, natural resources and every other thing is around, and all you need to do is create an environment and a framework that allows people to really maximise those potential. And we have never had leaders who did that. Chinua Achebe wrote a book

called *"The Problem with Nigeria"*, the first sentence there is "the problem with Nigeria is a problem with leadership".

Our leaders are so short-sighted, they don't care. If they have money, they will buy their own private planes or helicopters and they fly themselves all over the country instead of building the roads. If they feel sick or if their children or members of their family are ill, they bring them abroad for treatment, instead of developing the health service. They send their kids here to study, it costs about £9,000 or more for an overseas student at Goldsmiths. They send their kids to come to school here and meanwhile the education system in Nigeria is falling apart.

INTERVIEWER Did you feel there were big cultural differences when you came over from Nigeria the first time?
DR OSITA OKAGBUE Oh yes. I was lucky because I went straight to an international university in Leeds, which has always been associated with Africa, the Commonwealth. So I didn't feel too much of a culture shock when I arrived, except that one of the first things I noticed, was that it's only when you arrive here that you ask yourself maybe I'm not speaking good English or that's the first time you become aware of your accent.

The culture is totally different: one of the things I'm still struggling to get comfortable with is the relationship between me and my students. I remember not being able to call my supervisor by his first name. You get used to that, the fact that here my students call me by my first name. Here students actually know their rights, and if you don't come to class you're supposed to explain why you have not come to class. Go and ask a lecturer in Nigeria to explain to a student, the student wouldn't even dare ask. There are so many differences in relationships.

INTERVIEWER And your children, do they know about their heritage?
DR OSITA OKAGBUE Oh yes, they believe they are Nigerians. They speak Igbo language but poorly. We never sat down to teach them. We spoke it at home, my dad and my mum never sat me down to teach me Igbo, that's what people speak around me. So what we do here as much as possible is that we speak to them and we used to think that they didn't understand us very well, but they do.

We were under that misguided illusion that if you spoke your African language to your children, it would affect the way they speak English. But kids are very adaptable. We were surprised: the first time my kids went to Nigeria, they could understand pretty much what everybody else was saying. But we didn't say you are Nigerian, you are this or that. You are who you are. Identity is like the clothes that we put on at appropriate times and the children, the younger generations are very good at it. So they negotiate these identities much better than we do.

INTERVIEWER What about yourself, do you see yourself as Nigerian or British-Nigerian?
DR OSITA OKAGBUE I'm an Igbo man, first and foremost because I think in Igbo. I do not discriminate, I don't do any of those things. But I see the world first and foremost from my Igbo upbringing, my Igbo perspective but it doesn't make me parochial in any way. I am proud to be a Nigerian but I'm equally very, very proud to be an Igbo man. I negotiate those very comfortably.

INTERVIEWER Some of the people we have spoken to are calling for Nigeria to be separated. What's your take on it?
DR OSITA OKAGBUE I think it's too late now because if people are honest, there is a lot of fracturing that is already happening, so you cannot legitimately, even morally or emotionally, generate a sense of Igbo oneness that will sustain a country. I feel the time has gone. I know people still try to do certain things and I look at it and say it's a waste of time and energy, let's move on. I don't know who will feature in this new Biafra or this new Igbo

republic. Who? People from Bendel, Edo state, Delta state, Rivers state, Anambra, Imo? How many Igbo states do we have now? There are so many of them.

My wife grew up in Enugu and we bought land in Enugu and they are chasing us all over the place saying: "But how can you buy land here? How can you come and buy land, why didn't you buy land in Oka?" We say: "That's where we want to live, my wife grew up there and that's where she feels at home, if we want to build a house in Nigeria that's where we want to build a home". So much has happened, so much has happened now, and most of it has brought out a lot of divisions, a lot of tensions you know, and how do you negotiate those tensions now? How do you remove those things?

All we need is one good leader who will come out and say look here this is what we need to do. The human resource is not a problem, the natural resource is equally not a problem. All it needs is management. All we need first and foremost in Nigeria, is to train people who can manage our resources including our leaders, to look around and see what are the skills that people have, what are the natural resources that we have, how best to deploy these. To create an environment where people feel a sense of belonging. In Nigeria, the idea of national cake, is still pretty much what dominates our consciousness: I'm not going there because I want to create a ministry, or lead a ministry that will be exemplary in terms of its deliveries, but I'm just there to see what I can get for myself: how many of my people can I put into jobs, into key positions?

INTERVIEWER What about the Diaspora? What is their involvement?

DR OSITA OKAGBUE The whole aspect of Diaspora is that you are here and you're looking over there. That's what summarises Diaspora. My living in the UK for a long time, is not what has made me think the way I do, I have always thought like that. I have always been critical about the leadership, I've always seen it as a problem. Efficient management is what we lack. If we can institute that, I think that's the way forward. The country has to manage what we have, in order not to try to borrow from outside. It's the only way you know what you have, what the limitations are on what you have and then you know what you precisely need to borrow, or steal from outside if you need to, which is what Japan did. You don't wait for the West to come and give you their technology, they will not give it to you, but if you try to develop yours no matter how rudimentary, it is then you know what level you need to reach, and then you walk towards that. You can go and buy as many computers as you like and bring them back to Nigeria, if you do not maintain them they will break down within a year and then you're back to square one. The technicians, the technologists who will maintain those computers, who will look at these computers to see how to make them last longer in the tropics, those are the things we need to do. I used to make a joke with my wife, I used to say "we are lucky in Africa, in Nigeria in particular that our weather is not as bad as here. The cold can kill you but the heat cannot kill you; if we had heat that would kill people we, the Nigerians, would have developed air conditioners."

FOOD FOR THOUGHT
What can be the role of a poet or an artist in times of war?

Authoritarianism is the abandonment of freedom and integrity to an external authority. What can each of us do to prevent others from falling into authoritarianism?

Interview with Felix Odogwu

Felix Odogwu was born on August 5th, 1947 in Kano, in Northern Nigeria. He lives in Asaba and is a personnel manager for a Grand Hotel in Asaba.

Interviewer Can you tell us of your early memories in Nigeria?
Felix Odogwu I grew up in Kano. I attended my primary and secondary school in Kano, I lived there with my parents and I left when the civil war was about to start, to go to my hometown in South Asaba, now the Delta State of Asaba.

Interviewer At the time of the war what were you doing?
Felix Odogwu I had just finished high school, and I was about to go to university, but I did not proceed because of the war. I went back to university after the war.

Interviewer Could you tell me what were your memories of the war, when it started and during the war?
Felix Odogwu My memory about the war is not a very good one because when I was growing up as a young man, I saw many, many atrocities committed by the troops.

Interviewer What did you think of the government at the time of the war?
Felix Odogwu When the war broke out, the government did not do much.

They were bent on crushing the Biafrans. According to the government, the Biafrans were doing a rebellion and they had to crush it.

INTERVIEWER Could you give us an insight maybe into why that experience was that terrible?
FELIX ODOGWU I saw the Federal army, Federal troops brutalising the civilians. They brutalised them and made them do things by force, command them and so on. They had to do things against their wish. When the war actually started we weren't doing anything. We had nothing to do: no work, no source of living and no money. So I joined the army in July 1967. I went to the war front. I joined at the age of 22. I fought on the side of Biafra. We went to different war zones.

INTERVIEWER Do you think the Ojukwu Government was justified in going into war to fight for Biafra?
FELIX ODOGWU Actually the Ojukwu Government was justified because at that particular time the Igbo people had no other alternative than to secede. They felt they were not wanted in the country because of the way they were brutalised. A lot of genocide was committed against the Igbo people of Nigeria, so Ojukwu was justified to leave to create Biafra. The war continued for three years before the Federal government crushed the Biafran troops. The war came to an end early January 1970. When the war ended the rest of Nigeria embraced the Biafrans. After the war, the military President of Nigeria, the Head of State, Yakubu Gowon made a statement that there is no victor and no vanquished, that the Biafrans are accepted back to Nigeria.

INTERVIEWER What did you think of the propaganda during the war?
FELIX ODOGWU Propaganda on each side said they were ahead of the rest, to give hope to the fighting troops, that they have captured more areas.

INTERVIEWER What was your day-to-day life like as a solider?
FELIX ODOGWU The reason why I went into the army, is as I said earlier we didn't have anything to do, no food, no money. All I had to do was to go into the army and I'd get some money. My experience was not a very good one because of the horror: civilians were being killed. When the Federal army took a city, all they did is kill the people they meet. Because I had no choice I went into the army. Thank God, we survived. Unfortunately most of my friends were killed, so it was very painful. At the end of the war we counted our loses. The Biafran troops put up enough

resistance to have held the Federal army for three years. But the Nigerian troops were better equiped. The Biafran troops fought with what they had, they made their own guns, they made their own missiles, until they became assisted by some countries of the Western world. Some countries sold ammunition to them.

INTERVIEWER Did you ever feel that you were going to win the war?
FELIX ODOGWU I thought the Biafrans were going to win the war because of their determination and fighting spirit. I remember that in late 1967 when the war started they went 400 kilometres to capture Lagos, but along the line there was a sabotage against the Biafran people. Some of the Biafran troops were not convinced that there was a sabotage. They halted a few kilometres outside of Lagos. The advance was halted at Ore which is on the way to Lagos. The commanders did not advance any longer. They wanted the war to stop there, to end because of the suffering of the people. At that time Lagos was the capital of the country. And they believed that once they captured Lagos, the Federal army would be weak.

INTERVIEWER Could you tell us what your role was predominately?
FELIX ODOGWU First of all, I was tested in the war front. Once I attended about 2 to 3 zones, the commander recalled me to put me in a store, where I issued food for the army. I issued raw food for them to cook, and I actually remained there until the end of the war.

INTERVIEWER Was there a training in the army?
FELIX ODOGWU Yes, we trained before we started fighting. But the training did not take long, we trained for about a month before I took my keys and took my gun to fight. I hadn't handled a gun before but because I was desperate, because my parents, my brother and sisters were hungry, I went to join the army. As a solider, either you go and come back or you go and don't come back. I saw people dying and knew that one day it may be my turn. I summoned courage. Each time you wake up, you don't know what tomorrow will bring. Each time you wake up you don't know where you are going, whether you will go and come back with your mate or not. I took it as a sacrifice. Death will come to everybody some time so I took that into consideration before I went to war.

INTERVIEWER What did you think about the aid that was coming in?
FELIX ODOGWU The aids that came to Biafra at that time saved millions of Biafran lives. The aid came, food came in from many parts of the world

from England, France, Canada, America and that sustained the Biafran people until the end of the war.

When the Federal army entered Asaba they killed a lot of young men. If you go to Asaba today there is a mass grave. This is remembered by Asaba people every October. These young people were shot in the presence of their parents brutalised. When the Federal army came in, they were welcomed, the civilians welcomed them, and the next thing they did was they opened fire on them, on innocent civilians. A powerful Biafran officer came from Asaba. So when they came into Asaba they said that they had entered his hometown, and because he was so powerful, they had to massacre the people in Asaba. I think that is one of the reason why they killed more people in Asaba.

INTERVIEWER After the war, Ojuku left the country?
FELIX ODOGWU Ojuku left for the Ivory Coast to take refuge because the Ivory Coast government welcomed him during the time of the president Houphouët-Boigny. He flew out of the country and handed the command to his Second-in-Command. It is the Second-in-Command actually who surrendered to the Federal.

INTERVIEWER Do you remember their names, who they were?
FELIX ODOGWU The General who surrendered to the Federal troops was Philip Effiong. As soon as he surrendered, Yakubu Gowan, the president of Nigeria immediately received him with open hands, and then made an announcement, that this war has ended and there is no victor in the war, and there is no vanquished, so the Biafrans accepted.

INTERVIEWER But what did people think of Ojuku leaving at the time?
FELIX ODOGWU People were not happy that Ojuku left because the Biafran people felt that Ojuku disappointed them and abandoned them, he did not fight til the end. They were not happy because he took them to the war, but he did not finish.

INTERVIEWER Do you remember where you were when the war stopped or what was going on on that day?
FELIX ODOGWU On that day, our commander got a signal from the army head quarters and said that the war had ended, that everybody should put down their arms. But we were not so sure, because we thought it was another way of getting us by the Federal troops. Many people in the fighting line did not believe the war ended, but the next day, other people from

other fronts raised their guns up to signify the end of the war, so we were all relieved that it ended.

INTERVIEWER What was the morale like at the time?
FELIX ODOGWU Some people were happy and others were sad. Those who were sad were those who lost their loved ones. And those who were happy thanked God they survived. The army then would pull off our uniforms and we surrendered our guns. There was a place where we surrendered all our ammunition, fighting equipments and everything. And the army brought hundreds of vehicles to take us back to our various home towns.

INTERVIEWER So where did they bring you back to? To Asaba?
FELIX ODOGWU I did not join the war in Asaba, I joined the war in Biafra because Asaba fell to the Federal troops, so my family went to Biafra, for their safety. I joined the army in Biafra and when the war ended, each and every one of us were taken back to our homes.

INTERVIEWER After the war, did everyone come together to try and rebuild Nigeria?
FELIX ODOGWU There was a reconciliation, the Federal army helped a lot, for example in the area of food and medical to Biafra. The children of Biafran people went back to school. The Igbo people started rebuilding their lives again. Some people came out of the war with no money, no clothes. The Red Cross and other organisations in Nigeria at that time were sending clothes, blankets, medicines, water and so on. They also sent in many doctors to Biafra.

INTERVIEWER What was your own personal experience after the war?
FELIX ODOGWU War was not supposed to be fought in the first place. All those who lost their lives lost it for nothing. They could have sat down at a round table, and talk on how to avoid the war. Ojuku could have not gone to war in the first place, but because of the anger, the killing and the feeling that Biafrans were not wanted in the country, the war happened.

After the war, I went to school and finished college. I then found myself a job. Later, I went to study at university in France. I worked for a few years before I proceeded to France, where I had my first degree and then returned back to Nigeria.

INTERVIEWER Do you think Nigeria has developed since the war?
FELIX ODOGWU Yes. Compared to what I saw before the war and now,

there's been a lot of development in Nigeria. An example is the last election we just had: it was a very democratic and fair election. Although some people in the North did not accept defeat, all around the world people saw that it was the first time Nigeria did an election, and it was creditable.

INTERVIEWER What are your hopes and dreams for Nigeria's future?
FELIX ODOGWU My dreams and hopes for Nigeria is to see Nigeria as a very stable country and for it to be able to compete in the community of nations. I wish Nigeria to develop in technology, in education and medicine. My hope is for Nigeria to rank amongst the developed countries of the world.

INTERVIEWER From your own point of view as a solider, is there anything you would want to tell the younger generation? And also to the young people in the Diaspora?
FELIX ODOGWU I have to tell the younger people to, first of all, avoid going to war, and always know that there is the possibility of a round table conference. Nothing is worth people losing their temper and starting to fight.

I say to young people in the Diaspora that they are still Africans and that from time to time they can visit home, they can visit their country to catch up with what is going on there. I want them to always remember that they are from that side of the continent. They are here to get Western education and I am happy for the young people I have seen in London and elsewhere, that they are here assisting in the economy of this place. I see many young people in good professions, some of them are doctors, pharmacists, engineering accountants. I have seen them in all walks of life. I want to say I respect each and every one of them, and I want them to remain here and to abide by the law in their host country.

FOOD FOR THOUGHT
Do you agree that all political conflicts can be resolved through discussions and conferences?

It is difficult to separate persons from their ideas since people feel offended when their beliefs/opinions are criticized. Not to offend others, therefore, some people avoid dialogue. How can we overcome this obstacle in our search for dialogue?

Interview with Professor Herbert Ekwe-Ekwe

Professor Herbert Ekwe-Ekwe is an independent scholar who specialises on the rights of indigenous people and on the inclusiveness in state systems. He published *"Biafra Revisited"* on the Igbo genocide and will soon publish a new book entitled *"Readings from Reading: Essays on African Politics, Genocide and Literature"*.

Interviewer In the first chapter of your book, you compared the Igbo genocide to what happened to the Jews during the holocaust, and then you made reference to the UN and what they did. Could you explain what the UN did? What the foreign countries did, how they intervened and how they helped the Igbos during that time?

Prof Herbert Ekwe-Ekwe As I have argued in my work, particularly "Biafra Revisited", which I wrote to mark the 40th anniversary of the outbreak of the genocide, without Britain which was led by Harold Wilson as the Prime Minister, the Igbo genocide was a very unlikely event.

Britain was actively involved in all the stages of the genocide, right from 1966 until it ended in January 1970. They were involved in terms of diplomatic support, military support, advice, propaganda and in fact in terms of the role of ensuring the UN had a more limiting role in this particular conflict. In fact at some stage of the genocide Harold Wilson himself actually told the assistant, who worked in the State Department during the

Johnson administration, that he was quite prepared to allow the death - as he put it - of half a million Igbo people if it is what constituted the overrun of Igbo land. Such was the level, such was the in-depth level of British involvement in this catastrophe.

What was in fact striking, was that the Igbo genocide was the first opportunity for the international community to respond to the horrendous history that the world had gone through the previous twenty-five years, namely the murder of the Jews: 6 million Jews were murdered during the Jewish genocide or holocaust. Now when it came to the Igbos, astonishingly the United Nations hardly did anything; in fact the Secretary General of the UN during this particular period, a man called U Thant, who was in fact from Burma or contemporary Myanmar, made it very difficult - extraordinarily difficult - for the issue to be raised within the United Nations. Right from the beginning massacres in the North, it was shocking to see the nonchalant attitude of the UN.

The other point also which was shocking, was that the UN did not do anything even to rehabilitate the survivors of genocide who returned to East Nigeria. We often don't remember this: the East Nigerian government then which was led by Chukwuemeka Ojukwu, actually rehabilitated 1.5 million returnees as they were called, without any money emanating from abroad, not to talk of course from the perpetrators of the genocide, in other words the central government in Lagos. There were no handouts, no interventions elsewhere. The Ojukwu administration in Enugu actually rehabilitated these individuals, including civil servants, students, all the individuals who actually survived. But the point really was that the inability of the United Nations, was actually reinforced by the government in London, by the Harold Wilson administration, which actually was involved in the planning and execution of the genocide right from the word "go". There is no doubt about it; without British involvement in the genocide, it probably wouldn't have occurred. It would have been unlikely. This has to do with the whole politics that was underway in Nigeria, prior to the so-called departure of the British, because the British actually wanted a North Nigeria.

INTERVIEWER Could you tell us why Britain was so interested in Nigeria and give us an overview of how Nigeria was created by the British as you have said in your book?

PROF HERBERT EKWE-EKWE Britain, just like a band of conquerors of European states in the 19th century, played an important role in terms of this broad swoop of conquest across Africa. Nigeria, or that part of South West Central Africa, where you had varying African states, African nations,

African principalities, were overrun by this country called Britain and then were incorporated in the beginning of 1900's into what was then subsequently called Nigeria. There were varying nations, the Yoruba for instance in the Western part of this new edifice, Hausa, Fulani people. There were also the Igbo people, the Ibibio people, the Efik people, various nations and nationalities. All these peoples that I have mentioned would have had varying histories. For instance, the Hausa-Fulani were more monarchical, very centralised monarchical quasi-feudal systems that ran under the precepts of Islam. The Yoruba were also quasi-feudal, they had their obas and the kingdom. What was interesting was that the Igbo people were actually much more republican, they had more decentralised state systems. Some of them were what were regarded as city states, but more varied independent state systems, that actually didn't undergo the kind of centralisation one would have seen, either among the Yoruba or perhaps the Hausa-Fulani.

INTERVIEWER Could you tell us about the British influence in the Northern part of Nigeria?

PROF HERBERT EKWE-EKWE Well interestingly, one way of answering this is to indicate one point about the Igbo conquest for Britain. It was the most problematic out of all these. If you look at British conquest records, you'll find that the Igbo component was most problematic. It was not surprising that in Igbo land you saw the women uprising in 1929, and that came in at a critical juncture when it was very difficult to suppress the Igbo area. It is because of the nature of the political system the Igbos had. The Igbos did not have a centralised system, and one thing about conquest is that you have to centralise political order, so it was easier for the British to carry out that level of occupation in Yoruba land or Hausa-Fulani land, because all the British really needed was to attack a capital and then that state would fall with it.

Now, when you had more decentralised political systems like in the Igbo land, it was actually very difficult, because just a particular village, or a constellation of villages could actually form a state in that particular context. It was almost like everybody was actually involved in the kind of politics, that in fact the Greeks were dreaming of.

Subsequently, what in fact occurred was that you had a problematic relationship between the British and the Igbo people right from the start. In contrast to what actually happened in the North, the Hausa-Fulani emirs, emirates system were more welcoming, at least from the first phase of the British drive. They became, if you like, more incorporated into the system and as far as the British were concerned they actually constructed a hierarchy order. At the apex of this particular hierarchy, were in fact the Hausa-Fulani in the North.

Even though, one must note one area of contradiction, because if you look at the way the colonial system, the occupation, the enterprise was actually run, they had to rely quite often with the very dynamic hardworking Igbo people and the Yoruba people, in terms of the way the system itself worked, and that is why you found that in terms of the efficiency of the system, many of the Igbo would have worked on the railways, in the port authorities, in the postal services, in the aviation sector and elsewhere. So they had to rely on that particular dynamism. But when they were leaving, they actually felt they had to hand over the system to the Hausa-Fulani, who were obviously much more responsive to the British edifice.

INTERVIEWER How many Igbos were in the North at that time of the independence?

PROF HERBERT EKWE-EKWE About 1.8 to 2 million Igbo people would have lived in North Nigeria during this particular period.

They, quite often, ran an independent economy, they were business people, they ran schools, they ran hospitals because they weren't actually employed within the North regional administrative system. The North regional administrative system had actually barred the Igbos during this particular period from direct employment.

INTERVIEWER So the North was quite multicultural in a way, did the different communities integrate with each other?

PROF HERBERT EKWE-EKWE Not really, I wouldn't use the word integration, because the Igbos lived in what you call the Sabon Gari. The nearest is to call them townships, but they were not. They were just areas. The Yoruba, the Idoma, would also live in the Sabon Gari. The difference would be if some of the Yoruba, say they were Muslim, you might find them in some of the Hausa-Fulani neighbourhoods. But the Igbos definitely lived separately. Of course this arrangement would have disastrous consequences, because what it actually meant, was that during the genocide, it was actually very easy to isolate Igbo areas. I must also stress that there were Igbo pogroms prior to the genocide in 1966. Murders of Igbo people took place in 1945 and in 1953 during the British occupation.

INTERVIEWER Can you tell us a bit more about the period of time just before 1966, what occurred and who was in power?

PROF HERBERT EKWE-EKWE The so-called restoration of independence began on a very problematic note. The whole process of the restoration of independence, was driven by varying contradictions and differences of opinion. The Hausa-Fulani, I must stress, did not actually want independence. In fact, the intention of the North during this particular period, was that the only condition it could accept independence (and this obviously was encouraged by Britain), was that it had to lead the post-conquest administration. So during the last conference in 1958 in Lancaster House, in London, it was actually agreed. If you look at the elections, which were held in 1959 during the so-called dying days of the British administration, those elections were rigged in favour of the North, so the North administration, which was formed in 1960 emerged at the backdrop of this controversy, with the Igbos isolated and the Yorubas isolated.

INTERVIEWER Can you tell us how Gowon came into power? You wrote extensively in your book about him, how he did not support the Igbos in going back to the East, he didn't help them. And also, I believe there was a tribunal in June 1966, but nothing came from it?

PROF HERBERT EKWE-EKWE A lot of individuals who were involved in the coup were Igbo officers, but there were also people from other nations: from the Yoruba nation, from the Hausa-Fulani nation. But there were a lot of Igbos involved in the coup, and the people who also suppressed the coup itself were predominately Igbo officers.

Also, in Nigeria at this particular period, the most robust economy within the country was in fact East Nigeria. If you look at the number of people the Igbos were actually supplying: most of the country's scientists, most of the country's diplomats, most of the leading business people within the country, I mean, such was the level of human power that had been developed at this particular period. There was an investigation that looked into the coup, an investigation led by Hausa-Fulani officers. The people who were murdered in that particular coup were Hausa-Fulanis. The Prime Minister, a Hausa-Fulani was murdered, the Premier of North Nigeria was murdered; so, the point of the commission was to establish, if there was an attempt of the Igbos to takeover Nigeria. But was it an Igbo-orientated coup d'état because there were many Igbo officers who were in the coup?

Gowon himself was a member of this particular commission. The commission finished its report in April 1966, handed it over to the administration. There was no evidence that the Igbo itself as a nation, were involved in the coup d'état. Igbo officers and other officers were involved but there was no involvement of the nation. The Igbos had a robust economy: there would have been no reason for the Igbos to be involved in the

coup d'état, they wouldn't have gained anything from being involved in the coup d'état.

The conclusions of this particular study did not come as a surprise to anybody, but it nonetheless came as a shock to a lot of the Hausa-Fulani leaders, and also particularly to the British administration in Lagos. The British actually wanted the Igbos to be found culpable for the coup d'état. That is when, with this particular background, the British began to work very closely with Yakubu Gowon, who interestingly had been appointed Chief of Army staff by Ironsi. Yakubu Gowon actually worked with British intelligence, and it was quite clear that even before Ironsi, even before the administration had details of the findings of this commission, the British Embassy in Lagos actually had those details. Gowon and the British Embassy became very, very close, between January and July in coordinating the outbreak of the genocide in May, because the May genocide itself, the killings of the Igbo people, actually preceded the coup d'état that found Gowon ending up as Head of State.

INTERVIEWER How many Igbo people were killed at that time?
PROF HERBERT EKWE-EKWE 100,000 Igbo people were murdered between

May 29th and October 30th. This was the first phase of the genocide, so the genocide itself begun before Gowon took over power in July 29th, 1966.

The date - 29th - is very interesting because the whole series of the murders are the 29th of various months: we begin on May 29th, then another series of murders on June 29th, then on July 29th with the Gowon coup d'état, then there are the murders on August 29th and on September 29th, it moves to a horrendous Christendom with the massacres that occurred in Kano airport. These massacres are in fact captured by Chimamanda Ngozi Adichie's novel *"Half of a yellow son"*. So the 29th must be noted, you can see that it was actually pre-meditated, carefully planned. 100,000 peopled murdered during that time.

INTERVIEWER Where were you at the time?
PROF HERBERT EKWE-EKWE I was actually evacuated from the North when the murders began. My parents lived in a town called Bauchi in the North; I was evacuated to the East. We returned to the East as various members of the family. Nobody knew who actually survived. The entire family were in different places during this particular period. The northern most part of Northern Nigeria was about 400 miles from Igbo land. We escaped by different methods, and it would have taken months and different levels of organisation, which I examined in my book, *"Biafra Revisited"*. People were moving from different directions at different times, and of course during these moves, that's when people were unfortunately murdered, and most of those murders would have occurred for instance crossing the River Benue.

INTERVIEWER How old were you at the time?
PROF HERBERT EKWE-EKWE At the time of the genocide, I was thirteen years old.

INTERVIEWER What was going through your mind at the time, were you concerned about the safety of your family and yourself ?
PROF HERBERT EKWE-EKWE It was an incredible situation because I was at school when I was evacuated. I didn't know what happened to my parents. I didn't know what happened to my sisters. I was put on this mini-bus heading to the East. I was told quite clearly that there was no way we could go back to Bauchi, where my parents lived, because they didn't know whether they had survived. So I didn't know what happened to any of the members of my family, until I got to the East. But what was East? East was Enugu, but I didn't come from Enugu. I still had to travel another hundred

miles to my own home. As I arrived home, my parents were not there, I just met my grandparents.

INTERVIEWER Did you have to travel by yourself?
PROF HERBERT EKWE-EKWE No, thanks to the level of organisation by the East government headed by Ojukwu. The East Red Cross, and other volunteer organisations had already been set up. They documented that such individual, was registered, and they would find out where you're heading to and, if there were any individuals there who would actually be able to help you. They would also find out whether you were with your family. So I gave all the details of my own parents, where my father worked: he worked in the railways at this particular period. My mother worked as a business person and my other sisters were also in another boarding school. I had to give all this documentation, and then they arranged buses to take people to their own home towns.

INTERVIEWER How long until you saw your parents again?
PROF HERBERT EKWE-EKWE First of all, I saw my sister, who came through this process. In fact, my sister arrived through Cameroon, because during the evacuation she had been taken to the Adamawa province, which is a province that is contiguous to North West Cameroon; so she had gone through Cameroon, and from Cameroon she came down to the East via Bouya, through Calabar, and again the same process was occurring. It was an incredible level of documentation, and that is one of the reasons why the Igbo genocide became well documented. The Igbo government in Enugu during that period was carrying out all these levels of documentation. Later, as my mother came through Eha Maufu, she also went through this documentation, and had known that her son had come through two months earlier. She headed for her own home town, where we stayed and ultimately she saw our father.

INTERVIEWER Can you tell us about the propaganda used at that time? We watched a documentary by the BBC, and they said Ojukwu used a lot of propaganda to garner support from some of the British over here, and also from fellow Igbos to support the cause. Do you think this statement is true?
PROF HERBERT EKWE-EKWE I think it's pathetic to say the least. I mean the Igbos themselves survived. Anything up to 1.5 million would have survived and were coming in different directions. It was evident that a catastrophe had occurred. In a lot of images, there were headless bodies that came through. Some people were on the train and had been murdered

on the train. If you saw what was happening in Enugu railway stations, in terms of the documentation, it was horrendous. So it was very clear in the mind of individuals, that the concept Nigeria had ceased to exist. The fundamental role of a state, and I'm saying this as a political scientist, a political philosopher almost 51 years later, the issue is that everybody who survived this genocide whether they were living in Kano, Zaire or wherever, everybody knew that a calamity had happened to them. People had lost loved ones and lost possessions. It was a catastrophe, so the issue of whether one would continue within an edifice called Nigeria, was no longer in question. There were demonstrations that began in Enugu from October 1966 to May 1967. Biafran independence was not declared until almost 7 months later. One mustn't forget all the efforts the Igbo administration made in Aburi Ghana, to have a confederal system of governance. It was an incredible concession, given the calamity that had occurred.

The genocide was extended to Igbo land, on the 6th of July with an attack on the survivors. People had now, literally, abandoned what, then, was still, Nigeria. People had left the North, had left Lagos, Benin, Sapele and other areas and had now returned to Igbo land. By November, December 1966 it was said that an overwhelming majority of Igbo people were back. Biafra was not formally declared until the 30th of May 1967.

The Igbo administration, then the Ojukwu administration, called on Ghana to mediate. The Ghana administration, led by General Ankrah, invited Ojukwu and Gowon to Aburi for a conference. The Aburi accord was a fascinating piece of African mediation and diplomacy. 100,000 people had been murdered, in a brutal orgy of violence and you had these African neighbours, this Ghanaian administration calling on all the people involved for two, three-day meeting in Ghana, in this castle. They agreed towards a confederal system, which would ensure that people would live more autonomously. That was what was arranged for Nigeria by the Ghanaians. It was called the Aburi Accord. As soon as Gowon was back in Lagos, the British administration in Lagos intervened, and bore heavily on Gowon not to implement the Aburi Accord, because the British wanted an extension of the genocide to Igboland.

In June 1969, Nigeria destroyed an international Red Cross plane. It was the Nigerian third command marine led by Olusegun Obasanjo. Obasanjo himself, acknowledges this in his memoirs called *"My Command"*. He, himself, makes it very clear in his memoirs, that the Nigerian government headed by Gowon, had to rely on the British administration to "sort out" the mess created by the world revulsion, of the deliberate shooting down of this relief air craft.

INTERVIEWER You have spoken about the British involvement, also in your book, you speak about Russia, USSR at that time, who were also involved in supporting Nigeria. What countries supported Biafra?

PROF HERBERT EKWE-EKWE There were very few countries that supported Biafra, again thanks to the British diplomatic drive. There was no such confluence of the relationship between the Soviet Union and Britain, at the height of the cold war. For the Soviet Union, it was an opportunity to move into West Africa, and of course it wasn't doing anything that was wrong, because although it was supporting the genocidal administration in Lagos, it had its support from Britain. The Organisation of African Unity did not come out to oppose the genocide in any of its facets. In fact, the only people who opposed the genocide were people like Julius Nyerere, one of Africa's leading Pan-Africanists. He had come out clearly to indicate that unity cannot be imposed by force, that any kind of relationship has to be a voluntary relationship. Britain used its statute and power within the Commonwealth, to ensure there was no condemnation of the genocide within the Commonwealth.

INTERVIEWER How did the Biafrans, Igbos survive at the time? Did they have their own central bank, because we have heard that the Nigerian Government cut off any money coming to the East at that time?

PROF HERBERT EKWE-EKWE I think the Igbo survival is an incredible tale of the tenacity of the human spirit. For nearly 4 years, they were completely cut off, blockaded and continuously bombarded. The total fatality is 3.1 million. Even though they were being bombarded, they still published their newspaper, the *"Biafran Sun"*, still went out every morning. The Igbos ran their refineries. They also ran an efficient post office service during this period, they ran underground hospitals. The international aid organisations, especially those organisations that were centred around the church, were incredible in terms of what they did for the Igbo people. They were able to overcome the attempts by the Harold Wilson regime, to completely block the Igbo people. There were incredible stories of individuals who had formed organisations in Switzerland, in Germany, in Scandinavian countries, in Canada, in United States, in Italy and in many other countries to break the blockade. A French organisation called *Medicine Beyond Borders*, started off by a former French secretary, who was a young medical doctor, and knew that there were restrictions in place on the national Red Cross. So they began their own organisation to break the blockade. What was incredible was the human spirit, the level of organisation, which I think is why the Igbos were able to survive. There was an incredible level of optimism that went on throughout those savage months, especially during the entire period of 1969.

INTERVIEWER How were people entertained to keep up their optimism and high spirits? Were there any poets at the time or artists who spoke about Biafra's struggle?

PROF HERBERT EKWE-EKWE Extensively, yes. There were dramas, plays, dances, theatres, all kinds of operas were going on during this period. In terms of the poetry, Christopher Okigbo who continues to be Africa's leading poet was involved in the resistance. He died at the very early stages of the resistance unfortunately.

There were also other poets who were working within the contours of the Okigbo poetics, such as Kevin Echeruo, who is the younger brother of Michael Echeruo, a leading academic, who was for many years, professor of African American studies of literature at Syracuse University in the United States. Paul Ndu was also a poet. Many of these poets, who were writing poetry during this period, were exchanging. Some individuals, who were in their defensive positions, either at the front, were also writing poetry. So, it was intellectually, artistically an exciting period; trying to make sense of what life could be, in spite of the unsettlement, in spite of the bombardment. Igbo land was a very small area. The Igbo people had been compressed within at some stages 16 miles by 40 miles. People were boxed in there, but life still went on and lots of creativity went on.

INTERVIEWER At the end of the war, in 1970, was there the feeling of being defeated, or was there jubilation that the war had ended?

PROF HERBERT EKWE-EKWE I think there was incredulity in terms of what happened. Incredulity, mixed with the notion that might rules the world. There was also a feeling that people survived, and it was astonishing that people had survived. For a very long time after the war, the way Igbo people greeted each other was "happy survival". Anytime you met someone, you would say "happy survival mother", "happy survival Nna", "happy survival father"... So there was incredulity in terms of the fact one could have died. There was no sense of defeat, no. The Igbo didn't feel any form of defeat, the Igbo actually felt that through survival, they actually won that conflict - at worst, that Biafra had been deferred. The Biafra spirit continued via the reality that the Igbo people survived.

INTERVIEWER When did you move to the UK, was it just after the war?

Prof Herbert Ekwe-Ekwe No, after the collapse of Biafra, I continued school. I came to the UK to do graduate studies. For those who survived there was a secretion of Igbo assets. Any form of liquid capital was seized, bar £20. £20 were handed over to the Igbo male adults who had to certify that they were head of a family. And, we knew that where there were no survival male, that particular family did not have any £20.

For Igbo people it was the beginning all over again. Before 1966, the Igbo economy was one of the most robust economy in Nigeria. That economy was virtually destroyed. It has been allowed to degrade, infrastructures in the East have not been rehabilitated til today. It is what I describe as the third phase of the Igbo genocide, starting after the 12th of May and we are still in that phase. It goes contrary to Article 2 of the UN convention on genocide, where people are subjected within a particular environment, to ensure that people did not have the wherewithal to make life meaningful. My father survived the genocide, so my father was handed £20 and it was with those £20 that we began life all over again. I went to school and finished my first degree at the University of Ibadan, and then came to England for my PhD work.

Interviewer At the time when their properties were seized, did the Igbos go to Britain or America to start a new life?
Prof Herbert Ekwe-Ekwe Not many could do it. But some did and went off to the United States. Some went to France and some went to other African countries, especially those who were sympathetic to the Igbo people, such as Tanzania and Zambia for example. Some also went to the Ivory Coast, and from there, they went to France. But the majority of Igbo people stayed in Nigeria, and had to work through it. It was incredible the raft of discrimination they were subjected to. In terms of exam results, they introduced all types of quota systems, to ensure that you didn't have many Igbo people going to universities, although Igbos are very hard-working.

Interviewer Would you describe your identity as British, Nigerian or British-Nigerian?
Prof Herbert Ekwe-Ekwe I'm British.

Interviewer Despite British involvement in the Biafra war?
Prof Herbert Ekwe-Ekwe Yes, that's part of the contradiction, I could describe myself as British-Igbo individual but in terms of the passport I have, I am British, but I am an Igbo person as well, and I look forward to the restoration of Igbo independence.

INTERVIEWER You think that will happen?
PROF HERBERT EKWE-EKWE Oh yes, it will happen, yes. There's no doubt about that. It will happen.

INTERVIEWER Do you believe in one Nigeria?
PROF HERBERT EKWE-EKWE No, I don't. As far as I'm concerned, Nigeria failed to be a country, of any serious prospect, since 29th of May 1966. Nigeria has a particular responsibility to protect its people, but it murdered 3.1 million people of its own population. The way I see it, is that the Igbo indictment on this horrendous massacre, is that the Igbos ceased to be Nigerians on that particular day. Nigeria is one of these Berlin states, that was created by Europe. There is no future for these Berlin states. Africans cannot be continuously murdered in states, that do not ensure that they can actually materialise their own aspirations. I don't see any way that these states, as they exist at the moment, can actually help for the transformation of Africa, which I do see will actually occur in the future.

INTERVIEWER What are your dreams and hopes for Nigeria?
PROF HERBERT EKWE-EKWE In terms of the country that calls itself Nigeria, I hope that all the various principal nations that make up Nigeria can sit down in a conference. I wish them to sit down quietly, and decide for people to go on their own ways. I can see within a generation, successor states of Igbo people, Ijaw people, Yoruba people, Hausa-Fulani people transforming their societies, in a way that is actually unimaginable.

Let us not forget that the Igbo economy was almost on the verge of creating a China, a Taiwan or an India on the eve of the genocide. A future Africa of a Yoruba, Dodowa state, Hausa-Fulani state or an Edo state can, actually, be the bridges for a greater transformation, because these would have been states created by Africans, not by Europeans. What in fact is occurring at the moment is an awful haemorrhage. If you look at Nigeria, Nigeria still does what Britain wants it to do, Ivory Coast still does what France wants it to do, but not for the Yoruba, not for the Igbo, not for the Bulaka, not for the Wolof. That is the centre for the African Renaissance, that Africans urgently deserve.

INTERVIEWER What role does the Diaspora play? What can we do to aid the development of Nigeria?
PROF HERBERT EKWE-EKWE The African Diaspora is writing an incredible story. The African Diaspora sent more capital to Africa than any of the so-called aid that goes to Africa. A study carried out in 2003, shows the

African Diaspora, which totals about 15 million people in Europe, the Americas and elsewhere, sent back 200 billion US dollars to Africa. This money, fed by olders or parents, ensures that children go to school, that infrastructures are being renewed. At the moment people are funding schools, and libraries. Someone is earning some money somewhere; they could be working in an office, they could be a cleaner, they could be a university professor, they could be a medical doctor, they could be a journalist. And they all end up going to Western Union, to the post office, or to a bank and sending money, and that money makes a difference.

We have now moved into a situation where the Diaspora population are maintaining the infrastructure. It's an astounding story. Many things are happening in Africa at the moment. The new Africa is actually emerging from the old. The Berlin state has finished its work, if it ever had any particular work. It was actually a state which murdered Africans. A new state is emerging and will move Africa forward. That is where the African Diaspora population is playing a key role. If we look at what the Diaspora population is doing, in spite of the history, in spite of the broken society which emerged; they are working very hard. That gives us an idea of the African capacity, when the Diaspora and the human power converge.

FOOD FOR THOUGHT

Nothing is more barbarous than war. Nothing is more miserable than war. Yet war still drags on in many places around the globe. How can we make this century into a Century of Peace ?

According to you, what could be the role of the Nigerian Diaspora today?

Interview with Paul Lanipekun

Paul Lanipekun was born in Kano, Nigeria in 1946. He worked as a director of a housing association and is now retired in Brixton.

Interviewer Can you describe living in Nigeria before the Biafra war started?
Paul Lanipekun Nigeria was a nice place to live as a kid, there was so much happening. I was a child at the time of the Nigerian independence. Everyone thought it was great to have the British out. We, finally, had a government of our own. But, not long after that, the first coup took place. I was in the army, I am lucky to be standing here now because I was Stick Orderly for Aguiyi-Ironsi when he was in Zaire. Stick Orderly is a ceremonial bodyguard for the Head of State. I was standing behind him, and if they decided to kill him in Zaire, I would get the bullet first. He was shot the next day in Kaduna, as he was touring the country. There was a lot of killing which was actually one sided. The whole North was a blood bath, there were bodies everywhere, people amputated. They were going with the machete. The situation didn't normalise for weeks. And six months later, there was another coup. The situation then, became chaotic, because after the first coup, Aguiyi-Ironsi took over government as the Head of State. It

was another six months before the next coup, which was plotted by Yakubu Gowon. All the people from the East had to go to the Eastern part of Nigeria.

The relationship between Britain and Nigeria has always been one of business. I will give you an analogy "You have a man with an idea, and a man with money, guess who is going to end up with the idea and guess who is going to end up with the money?". That's what happened. The British Government saw clearly what was happening. I wonder why the United Nations is supporting the rebels in Libya, and they did not support Ojukwu. Why would they be putting so much effort into other countries, where they had no relationships whatsoever? But there is an on-going relationship between Nigeria and Britain. That's because there are resources that they wanted, British petroleum and all of that. When Ojukwu declared cessation from Nigeria, he made a brilliant speech, I listened to it, I totally agreed with him. If I was in his position, I would have done exactly the same thing.

INTERVIEWER What was his speech saying?

PAUL LANIPEKUN He was reiterating the sequence of events that happened. There had always been a situation where people in the South, I mean the Yorubas and the Igbos, they were always the functionaries of the Nigerian government. You will not find many Hausa people in Enugu, but you will find many Igbo people in Kaduna doing all kinds of things, you will find them doing government activities, you will find them in enterprises.

Britain provided the Nigerian conflict, it was all about selling arms and ammunition. Nigerian Army went from about 80,000 to a quarter of a million people in no time at all. They had guns, tanks, anti-aircraft guns, jet planes, jet fighters, war-ships, and everything was just dumped into the country. Nobody knew how to use them. So they had to fly a lot of people over here. The British army was training Nigerians. Naval officers, army officers, engineers were being trained. Even though we have a Defence Academy of our own, they shipped a lot of people over here to be trained.

That is how I first came to this country. I was in this country for 18 months under a programme. And later, in Nigeria, I was persuaded and hassled, but I said no, I am not going to remain under this atmosphere, and I packed my bag and came to Britain, and that's how I got here again. I have been living here since 1970.

INTERVIEWER Do you go back often?

PAUL LANIPEKUN No, I have never been back to Nigeria. Why haven't I been back to Nigeria? I ask myself that question so many times. Mainly because of family issues I suppose, and I didn't bother going back. That's 40 years. I became a British citizen, and I had no desire to go back there.

INTERVIEWER Do you have any connections with Nigeria at the moment?
PAUL LANIPEKUN Occasionally, I get letters, or a telephone call from people I know. I come from a very large family, hundreds and hundreds of us, so I still get people phoning up and saying "I am in London, can I come and visit you" or "I am coming to London" or "my daughter or son is coming to London", so I give them shelter for a day or two.

INTERVIEWER Just going back to what you said earlier when you became a British citizen, do you see yourself first as British or Nigerian?
PAUL LANIPEKUN I am a British citizen but of a Nigerian Heritage. I would say that I have quite fundamental reasons why I decided to do that. Carrying a Nigerian passport in Europe was a hassle for me then. I had to pay visas to go everywhere, and you are restricted to go anywhere. So, because I qualified to be a British citizen, I changed my nationality.

It was tough going in the early days, in the 70s and the 80s, in this country. Even for the nationals. Nobody had a flat, everybody had a room. Now everybody has a flat. If you were lucky to get a room and a job at the same time, you were doing really well. It couldn't go on the way it was going, so I started many actions. I became treasurer of the Federal of Black Housing Organisation. For many years, I was director of Positive Action for Training, an organisation which I set up, to provide training for black people in housing. We trained architects, surveyors, housing officers, because in the local authority you wouldn't see a black face. These days, if you go into a local authority, most likely, most of the housing officers are black people. The council was not housing black people, and that did not only apply to Nigerians: it applied to Caribbeans, all African immigrants who were in this country, and to some extent, some Irish people. It was difficult, so we started all kinds of things in order to change that situation.

We started that in the early 70s and 80s, and a lot of it has created an environment, where Nigerians were more part of the community. For instance in the 70s, nobody would think that there would be someone with Nigerian Heritage in the House of Lords. But it happened. Adebowale, he started in housing with me and he became a Lord. Or Chuka, who is MP for Streatham, his father was Nigerian, an Igbo. In terms of achievements, there are numerous people. Another example are the two world athletics who are gold medallists running for Britain. They are of Nigerian heritage. You can name so many people in different professions; doctors, lawyers, bankers, who are Nigerians.

Britain has been accommodating to an extent, because they value the input of some of us, and there are some people from our country who are doing unmentionable things, but there are some others who are doing very good work.

INTERVIEWER What do you think about the current state of Nigeria with the new government coming in?

PAUL LANIPEKUN Well, those are the types of things that contribute to my decision of not stepping foot in the place again. The looting of the state is huge. I was an army officer, and I know how much army salaries were, but for Gowon to accumulate millions of pounds, for the oil money that he has been taking commission from, and setting up a foundation so he cannot pay taxes or lose the money. There are so many of them who have looted the country, in so many different ways, and continue to do that. Some of them are doing it with the help of this country and of Europe.

But it isn't specific to Nigeria. It's a condition of human beings when they are put in a position of power, they are then likely to abuse their power. Some people are irresponsible, and have no interest for the nation other than their own personal interest, it is common everywhere, but the excesses of it is ridiculous. I cannot live and work in such an environment. If somebody wants to build a hospital, the hospital will cost 10 times the original sum.

INTERVIEWER Going back to the end of the war, what are your feelings about the end of the war?

PAUL LANIPEKUN I wasn't happy with the situation. I was one of the first people in the Third Marine Commando in Nigeria, headed by Adekunle, and there was no jubilation on my part. From the beginning to the end of it, there was no jubilation on my part. It hurts to see the waste of lives.

One day in Calabar, they just came with about twenty Triumph motorcycles, brand new ones. We all grabbed one. And a good friend of mine, Seun, grabbed one for himself, and it killed him. He, literally, smashed his own head on the street, and I gave the motorcycle back. I got a small Morris mini with no roof, just a bucket with a tarpaulin thing on it, and a small engine and four wheels. There had been all kinds of things in the country from lorries to Land Rovers – everything. That's the reason the country was so much in debt.

When I first came to this country, the Nigerian pound was more valuable than the British pound. Now you need a barrel, a wheelbarrow, to change Nigerian money to Pound Sterling. Those are the issues as far as I am concerned. How can a state that had so much, end up with so little? They were selling all of these Land Rovers, Triumphs. Ojukwu didn't have a Central Bank of Nigeria cheque book, but Gowon had it. It was a purely commercial situation, and they were buying not only armours and ammunitions. There were British policemen, British army officers, training and overseeing the activities. So it was selling anything they could sell and the people were buying anything they could buy. Everything was bought that could be bought, from fighter planes to warships to screws. That is one of the reasons the country almost went bankrupt.

INTERVIEWER You were fighting for the Federal government?
PAUL LANIPEKUN Yes. But I wasn't leaning against any side, you know as far as I am concerned, I manned the anti-aircraft in Calabar airport, Port Harcourt airport. I was just on watch. On a few occasions, the Biafrans had mercenary planes who would drop bombs in various places, but they were flying too high for my anti-aircraft gun to get anywhere near them. I would see the bullets go there *(points up)* and come back down again. Because I was part of that area of operation, I did not see what happened in Onitsha, in Enugu or the other parts of Nigeria.

INTERVIEWER Can you also describe the use of propaganda at the time?
PAUL LANIPEKUN The only propaganda that sticks to my mind was "To keep Nigeria one, is a task that must be done". That was Gowon's propaganda and everybody bought into it.

INTERVIEWER Did you hear anything from Ojukwu side?
PAUL LANIPEKUN The radio was saying all kinds of things, radio Biafra was saying all kinds of things about how successful they were. But it was ridiculous if you were in the know. According to my memory, they had probably a brigade of army in the East, three battalions compared to twenty, thirty brigades. They had no warship, we had warships. They had no fighter planes, we had tonnes of them. They had no reconnaissance planes, they had no bombers. The fight was no match, even though there was a lot of ground made by them, but it was lost.

INTERVIEWER Some people are of the view that Nigeria should separate. What is your opinion?
PAUL LANIPEKUN I think it shouldn't have been together in the first place. Here is where you blame Britain again. In Nigeria we used to rule by chief-

Paul Lanipekun with his daughter Dubheasa in 1998

taincies, kings, emirs. The Abas are different from the Jibus, just as the Ibibios are different from the Isekiri, and all of them have different chiefs and kings. This brings us back to the analogy that I gave you earlier: "If a man with an idea meets a man with money, guess who ends up with the idea, and who ends up with the money?". They came up with the idea of democracy, we bought it. They gave us a Federal state, a republic and wrote a constitution for us, they got rid of all the traditional rulers, and made them functionaries. And we thought we were going to have a democratic state but, within that, people were manipulating, and, when they couldn't get their way, it turned into a war.

I do not think that the North should be a whole country by itself because they could not sustain it, there is hardly anything there. There is no water, no petrol. But they built a refinery there, so they transport crude oil all the way from the Mid-West, or East straight into the North. No wonder people are breaking the place up and setting fire to it. We should build a refinery where the oil is. There are people in the Delta region, who could benefit substantially from the work that will come from the oil, that has been taken from their area. They are not being employed, they are not being educated, they still live in the same condition they were living so many years ago. No wonder they are picking up arms, whereas, some people are building skyscrapers and mansions for themselves in the middle of a desert.

You could put people together who have common heritage, who have common language if you like, even if the language is a dialect. For Yoruba for instance, someone from Jibu will be speaking Yoruba different to someone from Lagos, even though you know they are speaking Yoruba. Britain decided to take for instance, Cameroon out of Nigeria, because Cameroon and Niger were all part of Nigeria before. They took those small countries out. But if those small countries can exist how come Kaduna state, or Yoruba state, or Igbo state, could not exist by itself? The division of the country is part of why we are having the problems today. They band people together who have no common heritage, no common language, different moral values, and have different religion and of course war is going to break out all the time.

INTERVIEWER What are your hopes for Nigeria?
PAUL LANIPEKUN I hope that with the number of young people being educated and who have actually lived in other places in Europe, America and all of those places, we will find a situation where some of them will go back, and the governance will be different. They will not want to embezzle money for themselves, because they have seen the effect of it.

Nigerians are clever people, intelligent, well-educated people, capable people, but there are some people who think they are subhuman, all they want is to grab for themselves, and they think that they won't die, and eventually they die. Look at the last Head of State hanging onto power, until he was dead, and the last one before that, trying to change the constitution in order for him to remain in power. Those are the people who hopefully will end up in their graves, this is where they belong, and the new generations will come and make things better. That's my hope for Nigeria.

INTERVIEWER So you believe the Diaspora plays a big role in improving governance in Nigeria?
PAUL LANIPEKUN Of course, I strongly believe that. Unless that happens, there is no hope for the place. It is the children who have to come up with solutions, because they will see it's not sustainable. The ones that inherited all the assets, and what is in an entrenched position, will want to continue to enjoy the lifestyle that their grandfathers stole, but eventually it will change. I hope so. Probably not in my lifetime but it will change.

FOOD FOR THOUGHT

Do you think that people who have no common heritage, no common language, different moral values and different religions live peacefully together in one country?

Recognising and treasuring the contributions of older people is essential to the long-term flourishing of any society. Do you agree?

The older we are, the more willing we should be to listen to others, especially young people. Do you agree?

ACKNOWLEDGEMENTS

I would like to express my immense gratitude to all interviewees who have accepted to take part in this project - for their time, knowledge and generosity in sharing their individual life histories (and images) to a larger public. This book is theirs; it could not have existed without them.

I would like also to thank the Heritage Lottery Fund for their confidence in our team and their invaluable support to this project.

A special thanks to the committed working group for all their effort in researching, conducting, transcribing the interviews, sourcing pictures and information, providing the cover design, proof-reading... These amazing individuals are Bola Agbaje, Bisola Agbaje, Gemma Collinridge, Kemi David, Franko Figueiredo, Athina Fokidou, Chioma Ishiodu, Vera Janke, Kwong Loke, Muche Madhovi, Jennifer Maleghemi, Chuka Odogwu, Kola Oluwole, Ayo Osideinde, and Alan Stow.

Last but not the least, a huge thank you to StoneCrabs Theatre Company for giving me this fantastic opportunity to be the editor of this book.

Tanja Pagnuco

***

HERITAGE LOTTERY FUND using money raised through the National Lottery, the Heritage Lottery Fund (HLF) sustains and transforms a wide range of heritage for present and future generations to take part in, learn from and enjoy. From museums, parks and historic places to archaeology, natural environment and cultural traditions, it invests in every part of our diverse heritage. HLF has supported more than 30,000 projects allocating £4.5 million across the UK.

STONECRABS THEATRE COMPANY is a professional theatre company, incorporated in 2003, and granted Charity status in 2006. Based in South-East London, it works with international and diverse practitioners to bring challenging and informative work to the stage. StoneCrabs particularly aims to provide up-and-coming practitioners the support and space to develop their style, identity and voice while establishing themselves in the British theatre industry.

BOLA AGBAJE is an award-winning British playwright of Nigerian origin. Some of her works include *Gone Too Far!*, which was premiered at the Royal Court Theatre in London, in February 2007 and won the Laurence Olivier Award for Outstanding Achievement in an Affiliated Theatre (2008). Due to its success it was revived at a number of theatres in 2008, including Royal Court Theatre, Albany Theatre and Hackney Empire. Bola also won the Women of the Future Award in the Arts and Culture category, at the 'Women of the Future Awards' staged in association with Shell. She has also won the Best Playwright at the African Film Awards, and the Red Magazine Red's Hot Women Awards.

TANJA PAGNUCO is International Literary Associate at StoneCrabs Theatre Company and the King's Head Theatre. She works as a dramaturg to playwrights, a theatre translator and director. Her recent directing credits include: *Fit For Purpose* (The Pleasance, Edinburgh Festival), *Gerbils in a Glass Cage* (Tara Arts), *It's Raining in Barcelona* (The Cock Tavern Theatre), *Bar-Mitzvah Boy* (Oval House), *Memory* (Bell Pub), *Contractions* (The Albany).

***

NOTES, SOURCES & BIBLIOGRAPHY

NOTES
Page 9
1. Laitin, David D. *Hegemony and Culture: Politics and Religious Change among the Yorubas*. Chicago: The University of Chicago Press, 1986.
2. Ijeaku, Nmandi J O. *The Igbo and their Niger Delta Neighbor*. USA: Xlibris Corporation, 2009, page 25.

Page 10
3. Forsyth, Frederick. *Biafra Story*. London: Leo Cooper, 2001.
4. Chapman, Audrey. *Civil War in Nigeria*. USA: Midstream, 1968.

Page 11
5. Oliver, Roland and Atmore, Anthony. *Africa Since 1800*. UK: Cambridge University Press, 1994, page 270.

MAPS
Pages 12 and 13
Uwechue, Ralph. *Reflections on the Nigerian civil war*. New York: Africana Pub. Corp., 1971.

PICTURES
© Photographer: Romano Cagnoni, Hulton Archive, Collection Getty Images, pages 18 and 100
© AFP, Collection Getty Images, page 24
© Muche Madhovi, pages 17, 19, 25, 35, 41, 54, 60, 68, 79, 86, 101
© Hulton Archive, Collection Getty Images, pages 40 and 85
© AFP, Collection Getty Images, page 78
© Photographer: Romano Cagnoni, Hulton Archive, Collection Getty Images, page 67
© All other pictures originate from the corresponding interviewees

BIBLIOGRAPHY
Ikeda, Daisaku. *The Human Revolution*, Vol 1. UK: Weatherhill, 1994.
Ikeda, Daisaku. *For The Sake of Peace: Seven Paths to Global Harmony*. USA, Middleway Press, 2001.
Laitin, David D. *Hegemony and Culture: Politics and Religious Change among the Yorubas*. Chicago: The University of Chicago Press, 1986.

Ijeaku, Nmandi J O. *The Igbo and their Niger Delta Neighbor*. USA: Xlibris Corporation, 2009.
Forsyth, Frederick. *Biafra Story*. London: Leo Cooper, 2001.
Chapman, Audrey. *Civil War in Nigeria*. USA: Midstream, 1968.
Oliver, Roland and Atmore, Anthony. *Africa Since 1800*. UK: Cambridge University Press, 1994.